WHY GOVERNMENTAL AGENCIES UNDERPERFORM:
AN ANTHROPOLOGICAL PERSPECTIVE

How governmental agencies manage operational ecosystem changes

by
Dr. Julius Jones Jr, MMIS, DM.

Published by:
Light Switch Press
PO Box 272847
Fort Collins, CO 80527

Copyright © 2018
ISBN: 978-1-944255-78-7

Printed in the United States of America

ABSTRACT

The challenge of creating innovative programmatic solutions in many governmental agencies can be complicated by prevailing organizational cultures and predispositions for maintaining the status quo. The underlying question inherent in a case study of the largest county governmental agency in Minnesota examined the role of leadership in creating an organizational culture of change readiness. A culture that embraces opportunities presented by environmental disruptions and develops creative organizational structures to maintain basic securities (e.g., food, shelter, and healthcare) and public order for the citizen groups it governs. Governmental agencies exercise guardianship responsibility for its constituents by engaging its knowledge worker staff to enact operational structures and processes that establish and maintain standards of civil (e.g., courts and justice entities) and programmatic social service needs. It is within this context that governmental units must find innovative ways to reinvent itself to meet and anticipate the needs of constituent groups. The specific issue addressed in this book relates to the role of leadership in developing a culture that promotes innovative mechanisms for social and entitlement programs. Data was collected from 21 participants using focus groups and individual interviews, and analyzed using phenomenological reflection and imaginative variation to construct thematic portrayals of the leadership experience. The finding was that leadership is a critical success factor in creating an innovative workplace environment that embraces change through knowledge sharing, collaboration, and cooperation within its organizational ecosystem.

Keywords: Complexity theory, reinventing government, innovation, leadership, anthropology.

DEDICATION

To my wife Pamela Bandy, who has provided loving support for this long journey and for standing with me through of the up and downs that this journey presented. I also want to dedicate this writing to my late parents Roberta King Jones and Julius Jones who instilled a desire and quest for knowledge and the internal fortitude not to give up when faced with adversity. Also included in this dedication are my five children, Danielle, Julius III, Darius, Whitney, and Alora. As well as my 10 grandchildren, Kayla, Tyler, Julius IV, Daiwon, Jardon, Jovan, Barnard Jr, Daivion, Jailee, Brooklyn, and my great grandson Daniel, in the hope that my completion of this book might inspire them to seek out and complete their own good works.

ACKNOWLEDGMENTS

This journey could not have been undertaken or completed without the help of my Lord and Savior Jesus Christ. Throughout this process I have gotten comfort in the promise that "He who started a good work in you will be faithful to complete it" (Philippians 1:6). My faith has been a source of strength and has allowed me to overcome obstacles, push on, and stay in the fight until the final round.

TABLE OF CONTENTS

CHAPTER 1

Introduction

According to multiple academic and industry practitioner authors, the role of government is to exercise authority and control, administer public policy and programs, maintain basic security and public order, and respond to constituents' social needs. These social needs are the cornerstone of contemporary and historical tribal groupings that are designed to ensure the survival of a selected grouping and encompass a board set of specific expectations. Exercising this inherent authority directs governmental agencies to perform sets of duties consistent with the consent of those they govern and to protect certain rights widely held by a collective population or groups of individuals. During the exercise of its authority, government agencies work to enact policies to help maintain the general health and well-being of the governed body, which in turn directs the effective administration or operation of programs enacted to satisfy those public and social needs.

Governmental agencies discharge this guardianship responsibility for its citizens by establishing organizational structures and aligned agencies that enforce standards of civil behavior. Establishing law enforcement subsystems to enforce these standards of behaviors that have been normalized into existence and accepted as community values. These governmental entities also establish programmatic responses to maintaining standards of living for its resident populations and protection of its most vulnerable citizens (e.g., children and the disabled). It is this latter group that demands some level of commitment to public funding because the benefits of such spending. Broadly speaking, such commitments have been categorized as entitlement spending and has been the target of those who want to curtail such spending is favor of private sector or localized revenue streams (e.g., individual state/private funding). The theory has been for some sectors is that global or national funding for quality of life maintenance is readily apparent or provides global benefits to those providing federal dollars for those purposes. The prevailing narrative in global provision construct can be embodied in a Vulcan logical argument advanced by Star

Trek's Mr. Spock in that the needs of the many outweigh the needs of the few or the one. There is also biblical instruction on this point as well in that to whom much is given, much is expected. Governmental entities can be thought of as fulfilling the role, responsibilities and requirements of the narrative of global commitment to the provision of some level of social good and its inherent benefits to all members of a constituent group. Incumbent in the discharge of these role responsibilities is the requirement to communicate with and be responsive to its constituents over issues of the public good, which usually occurs during election cycles. This issue of what constitutes the "pubic good" is subject to much debate in various sectors of the population and can be influenced by countries outside of the United States. In many countries, public good extends from cradle to grave, and directs governments to develop programmatic responses to an everchanging basket of social needs. These needs can include healthcare, food security, housing and end-of-life services. These social needs are deemed to be necessary to ensure a reasonable quality of life and contribute to a productive society. In the course of fulfilling duties that serve the population they collectively govern; governmental agencies have the additional burden to formulate innovative responses to address the changing needs of their constituent population. Disruptions in the social landscape can make these needs a moving target because of the ecosystem quality of that environment. These disruptions can take the form of technology advances which changes the nature and composition of a workforce. Such a disruption can signal the demise of one industry and birth of another, which can affect the social fabric of an ecosystem environment. An example of this type of change could be seen in the fossil fuel industry which is starting to shift to renewable fuel and battery power. These changes require the acquisition of new skills in order to perform new job functions inherent to the new paradigm. In order to prepare workers for these new job openings could require intervention by pre/post-secondary education sector and public funding of the new training needed by the workforce. Currently, most post-secondary education in the United States is not funded as an item of public consumption, and those seeking this type of training must provide funding through personal funding or loans. This development in and of itself can cause massive shifts in wealth and income distribution because it can entail personal course corrections that require decisions evaluation of opportunity costs of one course of action versus another. The social ecosystem that all constituents are resident responds to a never-end-ing array of stimuli that interacts continual with the various ecosystem actors. These ecosystem actors can include societal norms, laws, regulations and popular opinion. Each of these actors can morph or devolve depending on paradigm shifts inherent in individual actor prominence and charism (e.g., political positional realignments). The social ecosystem seeks to maintain just the right balance between the various actors to achieve harmonious equilibrium and produce a reasonable state of well-being. This reasonable state of well-bring is critical to productive societies in that varying levels of happiness and contentment can be achieved. One of the more compelling ecosystem actor can be status related (e.g., income, citizenship, and/or educational). Another significant ecosystem actor relates to communication tendencies and preferences. As baby-boomers can remember, rotary dial phones were a standard communication vehicle along with written documents delivered in your physical mailbox in the front of your home. Nowadays, physical documents (i.e., snail-mail) are considered to be relics of the past, giving way to digital content delivered directly to a person using a personal area network (e.g., cell phone, IPad).

In terms of the most appropriate method of response mechanism to determine a constituent's desired level of societal well-being will depend on standards that those constituents establish as communication preferences. It is within this context that governmental units must continue to reinvent themselves to meet and anticipate the needs of their constituents. In order fulfill its role; governmental agencies must continually seek transformational opportunities for its operations, that are within the boundaries of its governance mandate. This is where the issue of ecosystem change management becomes an important organizational priority for leadership at all levels. Upper management establishes the overall strategic vision and determine the most appropriate direction that will achieve that vision. Subsequent management levels are charged with developing tactical operational response to the leadership vision and what objectives can be achieved in support of that vision. In most cases, public institutions such as government are not the most agile of organizations, especially compared to private sector entities. Consensus building around the most appropriate operational direction can be time-consuming in that overcoming objections to a prevailing operational narrative will most times meet resistance. That resistance can come from highly tenured members of the agency, or from established patterns of anthological behavior. This behavior can be pervasive in public institutions and can impede the type of transformational process required for meaningful change management.

This transformation or change process causes the most anxiety in a governmental organizational leadership, which can mean different approaches based on its management strata (i.e., upper, middle and lower levels) and how each level views and discharges its perceived duties. CEO leadership can articulate the organizational vision and determine the appropriate operational agenda based on board approved mission objectives, but the implementation is usually the responsibility of middle and lower level leaders to achieve that vision. In many governmental organizations, there is a lack of formal management expertise at these levels which can imperil the worthiest vision and in many cases run counter to that vision in a remarkable manner. The anthropological predisposition that is present in many public institutions manifest itself in the exercise of organizational memory about how the entity has responded in the past (i.e., that the way we've always done it). This anxiety is not however confined to governmental or public administration agencies but can also be a source of uncertainty for private corporations. Morris and Farrell (2007) noted the emergence of a new paradigm in the United States prompts leaders of multinational corporations to rethink governance structure both strategically and tactically. One such new paradigm has been a shift from a bureaucratic to what some call a post-bureaucratic organizational structure that features flatter management layers, shared decision making, and greater marketplace sensitivity (Lowe & Locke, 2008). The primary goal of the post-bureaucratic structure is to foster and promote innovative change on an organic organizational level.

The organic type of organizational structure has not seen wide acceptance in the U.S. government, but leaders in countries such as Australia, Great Britain, and New Zealand have taken the concepts under serious consideration (Crawford, Hasan, Warne, & Linger, 2009; Lowe & Locke, 2008). The social fabric and culture of many countries is quite different from the United States and is most notable in the construction of governmental health care and pension benefit systems. Such entitlement systems (e.g., medical benefits, retirement, and quality-of-life enhancements) provide the foundation of the middleclass in the United States and provide contentious debate for members of all parties in the American political system. The potential volatility of the political debate does not prohibit changes in the structure of these programs, but the underlying promises inherent to the middleclass require caution in the formulation and implementation of change initiatives (Marsh, 2008). This book is about the phenomenological effects of leadership behaviors that potentially allow for the successful completion of change initiatives and fostering an organizational culture that embraces innovation change through collaboration, cooperation, and knowledge sharing within knowledge worker communities of practice.

Background of this Book

Leaders of governmental, commercial, and civil organizations must confront issues in a changing social and economic environment as they move into the 21st century (Penn, 1997). One of the central components of these changes is the proliferation of information and knowledge that become the essential components of wealth creation and the expansion of intellectual and social capital (Crawford, et al, 2009). These social and economic changes cause an increase in organizational complexity, the operating landscape, and the resource transformation processes, such that they can destabilize the effectiveness of a management structure (Banutu-Gomez & Banutu-Gomez, 2007).

The salient notion or genesis of the structure question is that achieving cost-efficient administration of public resources and effective programmatic outcomes are tantamount to citizen satisfaction with governmental service delivery. Achieving citizen satisfaction is not the ultimate goal that forces other considerations such as social justice, democratic processes and oversight, the public good, ethics, or value-centric matters to irrelevance in the dynamic composition of public services. These other considerations simply add a layer of complexity to consider as part of the interactions of agents in the social network or fitness landscape.

According to Jun (2009), assumptions relative to efficiency, economy, and instrumental rationality fail to embrace the complexity of a phenomenon involving public consequence (e.g. social responsibility). Public consequence can be thought of in a cause and effect construct and serve as organic stimuli that promotes emergent behavior in governmental processes and tasks, leadership, and knowledge workers who reside in its ecosystem or landscape. Innovative change represents an emergent effect shown in the figure below that serves to stabilize and respond to changes in the post-bureaucratic landscape.

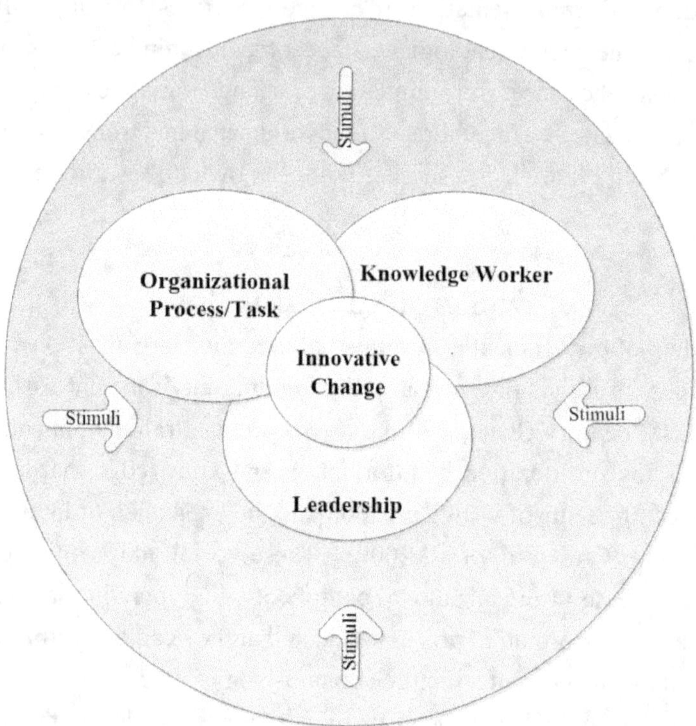

Governmental fitness landscape

Post-bureaucratic structures are a new organizational paradigm and represent a radical departure from a hierarchy and bureaucracy type multiagency structures with endless strata of management to a form characterized by the downsizing of the organization to focus on its core activities using fewer governance layers (Lowe & Locke, 2008). Post-bureaucratic structures include flatter and more responsive organizational structures as well as reengineering business processes that challenge the previously safe governmental career structure that has been in place for managers and workers. In the private sector, a mechanistic bureaucratic template is no longer suitable for the volatile marketplace conditions brought about by an intensely competitive international environment (Persson & Goldkuhl, 2010). Marketplace conditions are not as prevalent in the public arena, so the adoption of some post-bureaucratic features is not likely to be forthcoming in U.S. governments with entitlements such as health care, pensions, and long-term employment. That is not to say that leaders of governmental agencies should not embrace responsiveness to constituents and delivering effective services, but they must do so with thoughtful deliberation and planning (Pollitt, 2009).

The historical model of bureaucratic organizational structures in government produces silo mentalities that create impermeable vertical and horizontal boundaries that prohibit the implementation of changes in the organizational operating environment. The narrative incumbent in the new paradigm is that organizational leaders must think of an organization in more of an organic sense such that it reacts to changes in the environment in a manner similar to a living organism and that organizational subsystems (e.g., functional departments) resemble flexible membranes that react to forces in the environment (Alaa, 2009). Ashkenas, Ulrich, Jick, and Kerr, (2002) described the shape of these membranes as conforming in such a manner that the change does not compromise the structural integrity of the organism.

The conforming viewpoint advanced by Ashkenas et al (2002) indicated that the membranes serve as organizational boundaries but the pliability of these membranes in what these authors describe as a boundary-less organization in that such an entity enhances the flow of information, resources, ideas, and energy through its membranes to allow the organization as a whole to function more effectively. The function of most paradigms held out to be accepted models of operational behavior is that from an organizational leadership perspective it becomes an object that requires further articulation and specification in its response to new or more stringent environmental stimulus (Kuhn, 1996). Incumbent in Kuhn's description is the notion that change management is at the essence of many shifts in organizational paradigms necessitated by changes in the services provided to a constituent group. Central to successful change initiatives is recognition of the prevailing organizational culture, which defines the operational narrative and discourse of the entity (Ailon, 2008).

The problem context of this book resides in the delivery mechanism that supports the effective provision of governmental services incumbent in social needs, entitlement, and other programs for the resident population of this large county in Minnesota. The service delivery mechanism also extends to the partner relationships deployed in the delivery of those services. Prevailing economic conditions have resulted in the presence of constant tension between the need for governmental services, cost control inherent in the service delivery, and the effectiveness of the service provisions (Dawes, 2008).

Within the prevailing economic situation, it is a challenge for public policy-makers and administrators to discover innovative solutions that balance these competing needs and it is within this context that the problem exists (Marsh, 2008). Achieving creative and innovative solutions require leadership that is acutely aware of the environmental changes that disrupt the governmental ecosystems in which they operate. Awareness of the stimuli that exists in those ecosystems will allow leaders to develop operational strategies to manage change in an effective manner and achieve a level of change readiness for future change events (Desouza & Lin, 2011).

According to Jones (2010), the general notion of organizational change is a process which moves an organization from its present state to a desirable future state in an effort to improve the quality of its resource transformation process, gain or maintain market share, and do so with efficacy and cost-sensitivity. Traditionally, the criteria for organizational success includes an emphasis on role clarity, specialization, and process control, which is in contrast with new paradigm factors related to organizational speed, flexibility, process integration, and innovation (Jones, 2010). Organizational leaders seeking to shift to this new operational paradigm face the challenge of transforming existing enterprise structures and subsystems in such a way that the change does not endanger the organization's survival or cause service disruptions (Scherbaum & Dshemuchadse, 2008). Such a shift requires a strategic commitment from the organizational leadership to articulate, communicate, and tactically implement the new vision, but at the same time not completely abandoning its mechanistic structure in the process (Yan & Yan, 2010).

Butler and Allen (2008) noted two juxtaposed change levels can exist in any organization and these levels are in constant interaction. One level identified by Butler and Allen refers to mechanistic or surface change events and the other refers to a deeper or organic change and consideration of both levels must occur when implementing organizational change initiatives. This multilevel consideration is similar to the *neuroeconomics* approach to decision making that highlight the human behavioral construct incumbent in choosing a course of action (Scherbaum & Dshemuchadse, 2008). This behavioral construct advances a *desire-belief* (Marusis, 2010) model that posits a notion that people make decisions on the basis of what they want (desires) and how to achieve those wants (beliefs) in a rational confine. Decision rationality in this context indicates a cognitive discounting of a state of affairs relative to short and long-term conditions of satisfaction and the temporal distance between reward achievements (Marusis, 2010). Reconciling these perspectives and obtaining organizational commitment to a change initiative requires leaders to constantly stimulate willingness in landscape actors to trust and embrace organizational objectives (Brake, 2008).

Banutu-Gomez and Banutu-Gomez (2007) noted through the consensus-building process, commitment to change emerges not from the knowledge of objective facts but from the interactive building of relationships between people. It is incumbent on leaders to assess the level of organizational change that is appropriate for an enterprise by conducting an external scan to ensure that change initiatives meet the needs of critical stakeholders (Boyd, 2009). Leaders must develop an awareness of the type of change implementation and approach that generates positive staff behaviors and attitudes (Crawford, et al., 2009).

The overarching goal of any strategic or tactical organizational change is to reveal new or innovative ways to use enterprise resources and operational capacities to potentially enhance organizational capacity to generate service value to its stakeholder community. Organizational change most often targets four systematic levels: human resources, functional processes and tasks, technological capabilities, and organizational leadership (Scott & Davis, 2007).

Within human resources, organizational competences are inherent in the skill sets of the workforce. The skill sets provide for the creation of tactic and explicit knowledge, which can translate into competitive advantage for an enterprise if systems are in place to manage these knowledge components.

The leaders of an enterprise should continually review its organizational structure to determine if the knowledge workers in the workforce have sufficient motivation to use their skills to enhance the continuation of the organization (Davenport, 2005). Organizations must include professional training and skill enhancement initiatives to promote motivation and maintain proficiencies. Enterprises should also engage knowledge workers in the organizational socialization of the workforce (Brake, 2008). Introducing a new organizational culture could change the norms and values of the group to serve as a means to motivate a diverse and knowledge sharing workforce (Crawford, et al, 2009).

Functional processes and tasks refer to the manner in which the organizational leaders structure an organization to perform resource transformation work efforts and produce value. Organizational leadership can increase the value of its operational output by changing its structure, culture, and technology. For knowledge workers, these workplace changes direct the development of an organizational structure that recognizes the role that knowledge plays in the resource transformation process (e.g., complexity of work versus task interdependence) (Yan & Yan, 2010). A permeable departmental structure is an opportunity to engage workers to collaborate and cooperate across organizational boundaries to develop innovative solutions and responses to environmental disruptions (Ashkenas, et al, 2002).

Technological capabilities can change at an accelerated rate and the proliferation of new technologies can force organizational leaders to adopt new work processes as a requirement for staying competitive in their market space. The new processes can include the expanded use of collaboration tools for knowledge workers participating in the resource transformation effort (Kroenke, 2011). Deployment of technology tools can provide the enabling of effective responses to changes in organizational ecosystems. The adoption pace of new technology will differ by industry segment, and government is in a unique segment isolated from the volatility that inhibits the private sector. King and Cotterill (2007) noted constituent expectations are a driver for governmental agencies to adopt certain private sector communication mediums to interact with social concerns or issues (e.g., adopting social networking tools).

Organizational leadership capacities and capability achieved through the design of an organizational knowledge infrastructure and work culture allow the leaders of an enterprise to harness its human and functional resources to take advantage of prevailing technological opportunities (Brake, 2008). Knowledge engineering in an organization is critical because of the temporal constraints incumbent in a knowledge base, which requires constant refreshing of that knowledge to keep it current and relevant (Davenport, 2005). Developing and deploying an environment and culture that values each organizational team member provides the discourse that knowledge workers can embrace and internalize (Karp & Helgø, 2008). Such a culture fosters transactional trust among team members and promotes a learning environment that values collaboration, cooperation, and effective relationships (Brake, 2008).

These organizational change levels are interdependent and inseparable in terms of analytic examination. The most prudent approach might be to treat the organization as an ecosystem or organic entity so that any changes made at a subsystem level will affect the entire enterprise (Kira & Van Eijnatten, 2008). Governmental entities resemble a complex adaptive system that contains a number of loosely connected and interdependent subsystems that will evolve in unison if environmental stimuli force them far from equilibrium (Mischen & Jackson, 2008). Using organizational and environmental feedback loops, these complex adaptive system subsystems can self-organize and create new behavior pathways that adhere to a limited set of predefined possibilities that conform to the history, locality, and mission directives of the system (Arena, 2009).

In this emergent context, government agencies adapt to the challenges presented by their constituents by the social process of learning and in many cases by the political process. Such a level of organic change is in stark contrast to traditional organizational change theories that perpetuate closely held assumptions (e.g., reductionism, linear causality, and objective observation) that might exist in private industry (Bovaird, 2008). The application of complexity theory advances an ecosystem approach that assumes concepts of holism, mutual causality, and perspective observation (Ford, 2008).

These ecosystem concepts provide a perspective of the organizational change process as an perpetual, creative, and destabilizing, as opposed to episodic, routine, and stabilizing (Arena, 2009). Such an ecosystem approach allows an organization to deploy change initiatives in more of a grass-roots movement that emanates from the ground up and not as a top-down edict (Lichtenstein, et al, 2006). A bottom-up change approach creates less resistance in organizational subsystems because parts of the enterprise have a vested interest in producing desirable outcomes. The approach also allows a greater level of self-organization among organizational subsystems and the creative use of existing resources to generate emergent system properties and staff synergies (Lichtenstein et al, 2006).

Problems inherent to Government

The problem faced by leaders of many governmental agencies' is structuring service delivery models for social and entitlement programs to meet the needs of citizens within the programmatic reality of shrinking agency budgets (Walker, 2005). Leaders must balance competing demands within a governmental ecosystem to maintain structural stability of the system while responding to constituent needs. Leadership failure in that response can destabilize the system and disrupt operations of allied and ancillary organization systems (e.g., value chain partners). Structural considerations relate to the actual programmatic service and leadership functions that reside in the purview of an agency. The operational design aspects relate to the execution of those functions and determining the appropriate mix of internal and external resources to perform service delivery tasks (Robichau, 2011).

The specific problem is that the organizational culture in government agencies can present operational and leadership barriers to knowledge workers in determining cost-efficient, effective, and innovative service programs that respond appropriately and adapt to a mandated set of constituent social needs. Ancillary issues relating to the structural problem also extend to determining the appropriate mix of services offerings relative to constituents' changing life situations. These stimuli arise from a series of complex social variables that include the constituents receiving services and the government workforce having the task of executing programmatic policies and procedures in an ever-changing landscape.

Variables in the constituent side of this social transaction can include age, ethnicity, national origin, economic status, and culture. Governmental knowledge workforce variables can emulate many of those found in the constituent population but can include a different perspective. An example of workforce variables is worker age, which could be a limiting factor to reorganizing from a structure that uses in-person paper-based processes to virtual or technology-enhanced encounters to determine a constituent's eligibility for human service program offerings.

When viewed from the constituent's perspective, he or she will present a set of needs for which he or she expects to receive services or assistance to achieve or maintain a reasonable standard of living (e.g., meeting basic living needs). The human services delivery mechanism that satisfies constituent needs is less of a concern unless it involves an onerous or laborious process that does not produce a quality or desirable outcome. The governmental knowledge worker's perspective is in the programmatic efficacy of the service delivery process and the personal security of his or her operational role in the execution of that process (e.g., job mobility). Introducing changes in the operational execution of the delivery process can cause a disruption in a knowledge worker's reference frame if the change presents a future state inconsistent with his or her experiences. In this scenario, governmental knowledge workers may resist a change by seeking to maintain control or derailing the implementation of the change. This book uses a single case study research design to collect data related to decisions made by the county leadership in response to specific environmental changes in its governmental ecosystem. Data was collected from 21 purposively selected supervisory knowledge workers from the county in the State of Minnesota.

This book results might include insight into how knowledge workers in federal, state, and county governments in the United States can adopt a complex adaptive system methodology to assist in understanding how worker, constituent, and external organization variables can affect the implementation of strategies designed to enhance the delivery of programmatic services in a fitness landscape.

Purpose of this Book

The purpose of this book seeks to examine the operational (e.g., leadership behaviors) interactions and cultural factors of various programmatic actors (e.g., knowledge workers, residents, community partners, and community stakeholders) engaged in delivering programmatic service offerings and to explore how those interactive relationships precipitate in the deployment of service delivery mechanisms for governmental programs. The results from this book will indicate the complex adaptive system behavior of governmental agencies and provide an understanding of each actor's perspectives using a complexity theory model to assess the nonlinear effect that environmental changes have on each actor's operation and how the nonlinear effect forms the basis for subsystem self-organization to achieve desired outcomes. This book is based on a descriptive single case study design involving the study of operational models of organizational change as well as leadership behavior variables found in the largest local government agency in the state of Minnesota where change events are prevalent (Yin, 2009).

The descriptive theory the design encompasses is leadership behaviors relative to change events are the greater predictors of success and creating a culture of collaboration, cooperation, knowledge sharing, and innovation (Sarros & Cooper, 2008; Wong, 2010; Xu, Chen, Xie, Liu, Zheng, & Wang, 2006). Data was collected from 21 purposively selected county supervisory knowledge workers possessing five or more years of continuous county employment using a combination of focus group meetings, individual interviews, and direct participant observations. The logic of this sample size is reflective of the relevance each participant has to the research questions and change leadership concepts under study as opposed to representativeness to the study population (Schwandt, 2007; Yin, 2009). The selection criteria for participants in the sample was direct supervisory responsibilities, five or more years of continuous county employment, and involvement in one or more change related events (e.g., department reorganization or technology implementation).

The relevance each participant displays will be his or her perspective of the organizational decision-making and leadership behaviors relative to change initiatives. The basis of the chosen sample size reflects a representational mapping of the organizational structure that reflects the temporal, ritual, and routine features of the social and cultural phenomenon under study (Schwandt, 2007). To obtain corroboration of the data, it was triangulated with information obtained through focus group meetings, structured interviews, and participant-observations to ensure a convergence of the evidence of the role leadership has in fostering innovative change (Rubin, 2008; Yin, 2009).

The qualitative research design was appropriate because of the complexity that exists in each actor's response mechanism in the fitness landscape and the complex interactions that occur between actors during the service delivery process (Teisman & Klijn, 2008). Information regarding the role of complex adaptive systems can be useful in developing organizational culture change initiatives in U.S. governmental agencies that the results of this book could illuminate. Of particular note are the relationships occurring between the actors in response to the service provision opportunities presenting during public policy implementations.

Like many government agencies, the county also has several ongoing change initiatives, (e.g., knowledge management and transfer) that might lead to a future action research project with a focus on generational aspects relative to these change initiatives. Action research can be thought of as practitioner research in that it is a reflective investigation of an area of personal or professional interest, an operational problem, or an environmental challenge (Burnes, 2009; Neuman, 2005). Succession planning is one such challenge in that close to 60% of the county's workforce consists of members of the baby-boom generation who will be retiring between the years 2012 to 2017. Evolving to a workforce comprised of Generation X and Y workers might present challenges to the workplace environment and the execution of work efforts (Davenport, 2005; Page & Vella-Brodrick, 2009; Pratt, 2010).

Highly socialized Generation Y workers might present the biggest challenge in that technology tools are more prevalent in their daily lives and due to the expectation, that work has meaning. Generation Y workers are more hands-on and prefer frequent promotions and unambiguous workplaces. These workers require more concrete goal delineation than past generations (Neves, 2009; Page & Vella-Brodrick, 2009; Pratt, 2010). This book's goal is an articulation of predictive knowledge that can serve as an operational template for future change-related implementations by governmental agencies in Minnesota and other states (Masters, 1995).

Significance of this Book

The findings of this book might assist in the development of predictive organizational culture models and the development of innovative service delivery system configurations that respond best to the needs of similar constituent populations residing in other counties in the state of Minnesota. Development of similar governmental service delivery systems based on a complex adaptive system orientation can assist leaders in public administration settings outside of Minnesota that desire effective operations. The efficacy of any social services delivery model emerges by comparing and contrasting the existing social paradigm of the constituent population in need of those services. Changes in that paradigm can cause a destabilization of the fitness landscape and move it into the edge of chaos (Teisman & Klijn, 2008). Teisman and Klijn (2008) noted the critical significance of the actor relationship context using a fitness landscape metaphor, which represents the environment or ecosystem in which individuals exist, interact, and respond to stimulus.

Using the complex adaptive system concept, a fitness landscape will continually change because of the choices made by the individual actors. Teisman and Klijn (2008) explored the impact that complexity theory analysis can have in producing a governance structure more responsive to citizens' needs. The advancement of complexity theory as a means of programmatic development of public administrative agencies and services will fit in with the target population (i.e. county knowledge workers) because of the multifactor composition of the constituent landscape.

Complex adaptive systems are dynamic and in a continual exchange of forms, mechanisms, and energy that transition among conditions of order and chaos. Bloch (2005) compared phase transitions to the progression of water through its resident phases (e.g., liquid, solid, and steam). Change phase transitions provide opportunities for self-management, negotiation, innovation, and the creation of new structural configurations (Bloch, 2005). As a function of these phase transitions, actors in a complex adaptive system will establish a fitness peak, which is the point that gives that system the best odds for survival in its environmental landscape. Complexity theory is useful to focus attention on the evolution of phenomena such as policy, decision making, and institutional development as they relate to the changing nature of the actors' relationship as they react to environmental change events (e.g., new technology or regulations).

These change events cause new relationship models to emerge and self-organize in response to the pattern of behaviors currently experiencing disruption. This self-organizing occurs according to a set of prescribed enterprise rules or mission directives. This book involved an attempt to develop a predictive organizational model that can be sensitive to a constituent population's need for a particular set of services, or how proactively to address the present and future needs of a population group, based on its behavior and relationship characteristics. The predictive model will enable leaders to develop an effective service delivery strategic and tactical mechanism to address constituent needs dependent on the inherently complex relationship variables. An example of such a model would include response components interacting in a symbiotic relationship in terms of people, tools, and tasks process execution. The components of such a model would have knowledge workers engaging in the execution of mission-driven tasks with interaction between the relevant external stimulus (e.g., residents) and internal constraints (e.g., leadership).

Descriptive nature of this Book

This book is based on results from a qualitative single case study (Schwandt, 2007). Qualitative case studies are investigations and descriptions of conscious experience in its various forms and states, without giving preference to its state of existence or a judgment of whether that experience is objectively real (Creswell, 2007; Schwandt, 2007; Yin, 2009). The descriptive single case study research design involved studying organizational decisions about appropriate models of organizational change as well as leadership behavior variables found in a large county government agency in Minnesota where culture related change events can proliferate. Qualitative research is appropriate to assist researchers in gaining a holistic understanding of cultural ecosystems and the underlying narratives that guide actions and form the organizational discourse (Creswell, 2007; Neuman, 2005; Yin, 2009), in contrast to quantitative studies that establish causal or linear relationships to sets of operational variables. In quantitative studies, researchers do not factor in the substantial variability that can exist in independent actor behavior or decision-making process (Teisman & Klijn, 2008).

The deployment of this book might contribute to the development of a conceptual framework for evaluating changing patterns of social service needs. The conceptual framework could provide insights into the design of service interventions to provide the desired constituent outcomes and structuring an organizational management structure and organizational culture that best facilitates those outcomes. Attaining an understanding of the underlying complexity of matching services to needs could aid the development of methods to address how service delivery should occur in the population group under study (Wagenaar, 2007). The results of this book might assist in the development of organizational cultures that allow innovative service delivery models based on the interactions of complex actor relationship variables and the desired outcomes of those interactions.

According to Rubin, (2007), researchers who use qualitative studies seek to generate new insights, deeper understanding, and theoretically rich observations. Qualitative types of studies tend to deploy more flexible designs and subjective methods than do quantitative studies. Qualitative study outcomes help provide answers to evidence-based practice types of questions that have human behavior components that an investigator seeks to understand, which are present in the target population of this book (Creswell, 2007; Rubin, 2007; Schwandt, 2007).

Data was collected from 21 purposively selected county supervisory knowledge workers possessing five or more years of continuous employment with the county using a combination of three focus group meetings, nine individual interviews, and direct observations. This level of organizational tenure is consistent with the pace of organizational change at the County that has intensified is conjunction with changes occurring at State and Federal levels over the past 10 years (e.g., System Modernization Act). This book collected data relative to the experiences of a purposively selected group of knowledge professionals in the county to provide emerging leadership themes as the organization encounters cultural changes in its workplace environment relative to operational problem-solving. The change effects that can be found in the county may be similar to conditions in other localities, but extraneous considerations might lead to implementation differences. Issues relating to leadership, culture, and environment might be similar in context and scope (Mettler & Stonecash, 2008; Ostroff, 2006).

Conceptual Framework

The conceptual design for this book aligns well with the problem of determining the most appropriate organizational structure and cultural predisposition that allows the formation of cost-efficient delivery mechanisms that effectively meet the needs of citizens (Persson & Goldkuhl, 2010). Complexity theory is a vehicle for determining the extent and composition of social service needs as well as the organizational workforce relationships incumbent in those delivery objectives. The topic for this book is a complex adaptive system approach that recognizes the presence of a number of moving parts and behaviors that need reconciliation during organizational change initiatives (e.g., change and process management) (Persson & Goldkuhl, 2010).

Complex adaptive systems stand in contrast to ordered or chaotic systems in terms of the transactional relationship of the system and its agents (Ford, 2008). Ordered systems possess rule-based levels of constraint on their agent behavior, as opposed to unconstrained chaotic system agents (Kira & Van Eijnatten, 2008). Complex adaptive systems and the agents co-evolve because of light constraints on agent behavior, which can modify or reconfigure the system by virtue of relationship interactions (Teisman & Klijn, 2008). The results of this book might expand on prior cognitive research that focuses on social and cultural behavior patterns brought on by the interactions of governmental groups relative to public administration policy development (Arena, 2009; Barcan, 2009; Boden, Cox, & Nedeva, 2006). These complex and interactive behavior patterns can serve as predictors of the success of cultural change initiatives designed to promote the creation of an innovative and responsive workplace.

The emergence of self-organizing behaviors can determine the success or failure of an organizational change initiative (Nan, 2011). The self-organizing propensity is critical to explaining organizational behavior because it allows the connection of the touch points between interrelated knowledge management concepts, complexity theories, social network analysis, and application of these conceptions to an analysis of intra and inter-organizational policy initiatives (Mischen & Jackson, 2008). The case study design of this book includes data collection from organizational documents (e.g., project plans, feasibility studies, focus groups, and surveys), interviews with organizational leaders, and interviews of selected policymakers (e.g., county commissioners).

Analysis of the data collected might result in the detection of critical success factors (e.g., leadership) that can serve as outcome predictors for any cultural change initiative under consideration. The outcomes from this book might contribute to the body of knowledge through a framework that could allow organizational leaders to determine if achieving an innovative enterprise workplace solution requires an understanding of the social networks, cultural value dimensions, and their role in organizational operations and its interaction with constituents. Organizational leaders should also understand the behavior routines that emerge from those networks and how these affect the fitness landscapes (Teisman & Klijn, 2008).

An essential component of any fitness landscape is the influence of organizational knowledge workers who deploy tacit and explicit knowledge to meet the needs of citizens. Changes in a knowledge worker's workplace environment can adversely disrupt the service delivery mechanism if value dimensions infractions create uncertainty and mistrust in an organization's work systems (Davenport, 2005; Robert, Dennis, & Hung, 2009). Leaders must be aware of the harm a lack of transactional trust and attention to cultural value dimension can have in an organizational team structure and how that mistrust will stifle worker creativity and innovation (Brake, 2008).

Definitions

Actor: Any entity (e.g., individual, group, agent, or business) that exists in a public administration environment that behaves according to predefined laws, principles, or self-interest. Actors have self-organizing capacities within a consolidated whole of a larger entity and develop at an unpredictable rate (Teisman & Klijn, 2008).

Autopoiesis: This state defines a social system as a self-replicating communication entity. The implication is that a biological system is autopoietic because its means of production and reproduction are self-contained, autonomous, bounded, and self-generating. The system components have specific properties and its behavior emerges through an interactive process between those components (Alaa, 2009).

Complex adaptive system: A type of complex system representing diverse and interconnected elements that can adapt and change in response to experience. Complex adaptive systems can include systems such as the stock market, insect colonies, a biosphere, an ecosystem, the human body, a manufacturing concern, or any societal group endeavor residing in a collective culture or social system such as political parties or population segment (Bloch, 2005).

Complexity Theory: Any set of concepts that seeks to explain phenomenon that is not explainable using mechanistic or causal theories. The complexity theory incorporates contributions from chaos theory, cognitive psychology, computer science, evolutionary biology, general systems theory, fuzzy logic, information theory, and other natural or artificial systems. The theory posits that complex behavior can emerge from static and simple constraints, but that behavior occurs in a nonlinear configuration (Aydinoglu, 2010).

Fitness landscape: A metaphor that describes the environment or surrounding in which a collection of actors exists, interact, and behave. The metaphor description is used to generate insights into the interactive patterns and relationship behaviors between actors and environmental constrains (e.g., rules, decisions, or disruptions) that occur in those settings (Teisman & Klijn, 2008).

Holon: A term synonymous with system that refers to the concept of system thinking that differentiates machine (hard) systems thinking from human (soft) systems thinking. The distinction separating hard and soft systems thinking is that the focus of hard systems thinking is more on the engineering aspects of system dynamics whereas soft systems thinking has more of a human psychology focus (Yan & Yan, 2010).

Innovation: Joseph A. Schumpeter coined the phrase "creative destruction" to describe innovation, which he and others agree represent the introduction of new products, new methods of production, or the opening of new markets (Brcar & Lah, 2011; Danylkiv, 2013; Jonsdottir, 2013; Spangenburg, 2014). This definition advanced innovation as a process as opposed to an object of articulation or end state. As a process, innovation occurs when accumulated *innovative* changes come to fruition and produce a final operational result or product. Danylkiv (2013) characterized innovation as a socio-techno-economic process, through which the practical application of ideas and inventions create better programmatic outcomes, products, increased market share, or enhanced profits.

Innovative: Brcar and Lah, (2011) advanced the notion that innovation as a process results from innovative (i.e., creative) ideas that evolved over time, gradually and consistently specified, transformed from the abstract to the real, understood and materialized. Bassiti and Ajhoun, (2013) noted that innovation begins with creative ideas and the core definition of creativity is the ability to produce novel or unanticipated workflow products that are high in quality and usefulness. Creativity is also defined as an ability to imagine or invent something new or generate new ideas by combining, changing, or reapplication of existing ideas, as well as an attitude or orientation to accept change and new operational modalities, willingness to experiment with ideas, and a flexible outlook (Antonelli, 2013; Brcar & Lah, 2011; Pervez, Maritz, & Waal, 2014).

Neuroeconomics: A term that refers to a branch of economics that involves a search to comprehend the neural foundation of individual choice behavior and its core processes, which are thought to be similar to simple sensory or complex economic decisions (Scherbaum & Dshemuchadse, 2008).

Quanxi: The basis of Chinese culture that divides life philosophy into realism, idealism, and transcendentalism subparts. Realism has a basis in mutual material gain, idealism has a basis in morality and oneness with nature and transcendentalism refers to self-realization and personality to establish an ideal society (Wong, 2010).

Transactional trust: A concept that refers to enhancing organizational team effectiveness by establishing a set of ground rules for group interactions using a TRADITIONS framework (i.e. technological competence, results orientation, accountability, discipline, initiative, time management, interpersonal effectiveness, openness, networking, and self-sufficiency (Brake, 2008)

Assumptions

The validity of certain assumptions is necessary for the case study to provide a meaningful inspection of the topic of change management in governmental agencies. One such assumption is that responses to focus group questions will produce truthful and accurate representations of participants' experience with the topic under study. The possibility of bias might exist because of organizational affiliation, but a mitigation strategy can help to address this issue through the participant selection process and data validation methods (Neuman, 2005; Rubin, 2008; Yin, 2009).

A second assumption is that the focus groups and interviews will capture cross-sectional data representing the county supervisory knowledge workers' reactions to change in an organization. A third assumption relates to the second assumption in that focus group and interview questions will provide reasonable evidence of the topic under consideration (Schwandt, 2007). The fourth assumption relates to the appropriateness of the qualitative study design for articulating participant experience with the topic relating to change events and underlying cause or stimuli (Neuman, 2005; Schwandt, 2007). A fifth assumption is that data collected from the focus group and structured interviews will yield similar results (Chorba, 2011; Rubin, 2008).

Scope, Limitations, and Delimitations

This book's scope was bound to the spatial experience and perceptions of the county knowledge workers relating to change events and the temporal constraints of those events. The study perimeters were the largest county government in Minnesota and included a cross-section of staff to represent generational and organizational level (e.g., upper, middle, and line managers). The selection perimeters were confined to the supervisory levels of the knowledge worker population in the county that have greater than five years of employment with the county. Governmental programmatic actions can be thought of as path dependent and as such follow a linear pattern (Barcan, 2009; Pollitt, 2009). Tenure in an agency would indicate a level of experience that is predicated on knowledge of this longitudinal agency behavior. This book's primary limitation related to the selection of staff to participate in the study and their provision of open and honest responses. Another limitation was the location of the focus group and interviews that will occur at county-owned facilities in Minneapolis rather than a neutral site. A third limitation related to the single case study format of this book that will provide episodic results that might change over time under different circumstances.

An additional limitation relates to the execution of this book by a researcher who is also an employee of the county and the possibility of participatory bias in data collection and analysis activities. The mitigation strategy for this limitation is that personal involvement in these change events was on a peripheral level and that participation had no effect or investment in one outcome versus another. Neuman, (2005) advanced the issue of bias as an omnipresent event in social science research and noted that qualitative researchers emphasize a priori knowledge of the research environment under study. Neuman also noted that this situation allows the research to take advantage of intimate personal insight, feelings, and human perspectives to gain a comprehensive understanding of social life (Baxter & Jack, 2008; Chorba, 2011; Neuman, 2005).

The primary delimitation is the data collection timeframe and the occurrence of the change events. Potential participants in this book might be the victims of stress or apprehension about change events that could affect their perceptions and reactions to those changes. The temporal delimitation of the data collection effort resulted in selecting knowledge workers with management or supervisory responsibilities. These temporal and worker experience factors might negatively affect the generalizability of the results of this book to the other 86 counties in Minnesota and also to dissimilar size counties in other states.

Summary

The problem of social program design can morph into a seemingly endless morass of complex relationships and interactive events that have the potential to produce unpredictable outcomes (Liou & Korosec, 2009). Complexity theory can apply to the study of governmental systems in that these relationships can dictate the manner in which structure will evolve from the behavior patterns of the actors inhabiting the fitness landscape that bound its ecosystem (Teisman & Klijn, 2008). Much like an organic organism, governmental agencies can resemble complex adaptive systems that respond to external and internal stimuli and self-organize to address destabilizing change events (e.g., budget cuts and increased demand for services). The response to destabilization requires innovation by knowledge workers and leaders to create the conditions that allow a culture of knowledge sharing, collaboration, and cooperation to achieve innovation.

The literature review that follows in the next chapter contains highlights of some of those change events in government operations. Key to understanding the complexities of change that occurs in governmental agencies is that the relationships emerge in unison and are analytically inseparable. The change events that occur serve as catalysts for actor interactions that produce a nonlinear effect that can defy prediction. The literature is extensive on the chronology of various change agents (e.g., paperwork reduction, enterprise resource planning, performance measures, and the Year 2000 [Y2K] problem) but what is not easily discoverable is the complexity of the interactions relating to constituents, workers, and external organizations, which will be the major contribution from this book to the field.

Chapter 2

Chronological Review of existing Literature

The literature available for the change management topic is extensive and has relevance to social science and organizational studies. The psychology of change and self-organizing behavior is also prevalent in much of the literature. In a future study, a researcher could determine the interconnectedness of the change phenomenon to most ecosystems. The extensive coverage devoted to this topic relates to its role as economic and cultural stimuli that interact in an ecosystem to produce an instability or chaos.

At least three primary components exist in an organizational workflow (i.e. people, tools, and tasks). Each component reacts independently to a change event or disruption and works in a rational sequence to restore equilibrium. Complexity theory is a means to visualize and ultimately predict how innovative change emerges from a group response to chaos situations (Amblard, 2007; Bloch, 2005). The prevailing sociopolitical stimulus that exists in the governmental ecosystem (e.g., country, state, county, or municipality) produces a direct action that alters service delivery workflows (Robichau, 2011).

The exact configuration changes to the workflow component depend on the series of interactions that occurs in the ecosystem and the direction of the behavioral shift in response to various environmental stimuli. The shift that occurs can follow how constituents believe government should discharge its role and whether the government is anarchist, totalitarian, or something in between those extremes (Lipford & Slice, 2007). An anarchist in one who believes there should be no government, in contrast to a totalitarian socialist who believes in complete state control of an economy and its society (Lipford & Slice, 2007). At a minimum the form of government that emerges from the ecosystem stimulation should establish configurations of law and order, foster growth enhancing policies, and provide for the public good.

Constituent involvement provides a mechanism to achieve a level of accountability for government to ensure that citizens adhere to these ideals (King & Cotterill, 2007). Both the Clinton and the George W. Bush administrations held accountability as a primary condition of satisfaction for government operations and acceptable performance became a benchmark that agency leaders were to develop as organizational metrics (Posner, 2007). The notion of governmental performance metrics is not a new concept, extensive literature exists about this topic and performance improvement has been the crux for change initiatives in governmental agencies (Arena, 2009; Bellamy, 2010; Jones & McCaffery, 2010). Change readiness of government is dependent on multiple factors relating to the organizational culture and leadership that provide the greater predictors of successfully implementing changes that enhance organizational performance (Boden, Cox, & Nedeva, 2006).

Thompson (2006) described this phenomenon as civil service logic of action in that institutional rules define organizational behavior and establishes norms that guide decision making. Such a logic model would direct public servants to behave in ways consistent with group or individual patterns of subjective responsibility, as opposed to the instrumental dimensions of work (Thompson, 2006). The instrumental dimension of work is an essential component to the enhancement of the governmental performance paradigm. Change management as a practice is the subject of extensive research, but for purposes of this book, the majority of the selected material centers on the complexity inherent in deploying change in government.

The literature search terms represent components that affect the change management process or the organizational structure that dictate one approach versus another. The change management phenomenon will manifest differently in a bureaucratic enterprise than in a post-bureaucratic organizational structure (Lowe & Locke, 2008). Bureaucracies generally direct change initiatives in a rational and mechanistic top-down direction in contrast to a more organic bottom-up post-bureaucratic organization (Pollitt, 2009). The public administration arena resembles a complex adaptive system in that a landscape of actors interacts and forms relationships to discharge functions that benefit the social well-being of a group (Shin, 2006).

These relationships form around a set of objectives mutually agreed to for the promotion of cost-efficient and effective service provision (Long & Spurlock, 2008). In a complex adaptive system, these objectives emerge in a self-organizing manner that maintains or regains equilibrium in the system. Key to these relationships is the presence of common beliefs and unity in discourse that provide the basis for group decision making (Ailon, 2008). From a philosophical perspective, one could posit that an individual makes decisions on the basis of what he or she desires or wants and the belief of how best to achieve those desires (Marusis, 2010; Scherbaum & Dshemuchadse, 2008).

People form alliances with others of like minds as a means of advancing objectives and goals that ultimately benefit the whole group. Table 1 shows a summary of the information resources available from University of Phoenix Library electronic resources, Internet resources such a Google Scholar and online psychology databases that relate to the narrow focus of the study.

Search Terms for Literature Review

Search term	Peer-reviewed articles	Dissertations	Electronic books
Bureaucratic organization	520	5	5
Change management	250	15	2
Chaordic leadership	85	0	0
Chaos theory	120	20	0
Complex adaptive systems	150	3	0
Complexity theory	350	20	2
Enterprise resource planning	320	15	3
Innovation management	250	15	10
Knowledge engineering	250	50	50
Paperwork Reduction Act	525	10	15
Post-bureaucratic organization	540	25	5
Public administration	500	50	5
Transformational leadership	801	18	5

The representative sample of the literature available on topics relating to change management and the inherent complexity in an organization's response to disruptions in its ecosystem contains a variety of organizational design considerations. The apparent deficiency in the literature is an exploration of the nonlinear effect of complex adaptive system thinking and its contributions to the application of normal science experiments relating to the short and long-term behavior of actors to change events. A search of the literature revealed that change is a constant in most organizational environments and the appropriate mechanisms must be in place to allow those entities to respond to change in a predictive manner. The literature also highlighted the structural preference that organizational leaders have taken to position the enterprise to respond to instability in its operational environment. A common theme that emerged from the literature is a concern for the ability of organizational leaders to respond to environmental changes in the ecosystem or fitness landscape of an organization.

Organizational leaders' response to change will sometimes result in a reorganization to accelerate the rate of change, which can produce a disturbance in the status quo or a threat to job security and upsets the organizational discourse (Barcan, 2009). People will resist change for several reasons, but a primary consideration is misunderstanding of the change implications and a perception that compliance cost will exceed personal gain (Kotter & Schlesinger, 2008). Selection of the most pertinence literature sources were those dealing with governmental operation in developed countries with highly complex economies. Service-oriented government is a concept popular with Chinese scholars that advances the notion that the organization of government occurs through legal procedures under the guidance of citizen and society-centering concepts to ensure that social responsibility is inherent in the operational framework of a social democracy (Gang, Shu-tao, & Qiang, 2009).

The conceptual definition of citizen and society-centering nature encompasses the inherent characteristics of governmental work and the goal of pursuing the interests of constituents and society (Gang, et al, 2009; Wong, 2010). King and Cotterill (2007) offered another example of adherence to the voices of citizens relating to the structure and accessibility of public service offerings in the United Kingdom. Citizen participation and engagement represent critical components in the structure of governance, community development, decision making, communication, citizen empowerment, and knowledge sharing (King & Cotterill, 2007). The conceptual framework inherent in the Chinese and British examples is similar to what is prevalent in most countries, which is the rejection of anarchy as an ideal governance model.

Establishing a set of ethical rules enhances the probability of success in such a scenario, but those rules provide no guarantee as to sufficiency in the provision of societal order, without which the social group can deteriorate into a chaotic and lawless state (Lipford & Slice, 2007). The selection of private sector resources is a contrast to public sector agencies in the areas of performance, motivation, knowledge sharing, cooperation, and collaboration. These areas are common to most organizations, but the stakeholder group manifest different sets of expectations in terms of desirable outcomes. Kotter and Schlesinger (2008) noted this commonality as a lack of trust between the change initiator and employees, which can be attributable to the inability of management to change attitudes and behaviors to accommodate organizational needs.

Managers might understand the need for change on an intellectual or operational level, but their proclivity to avoid change can render them emotionally incapable of making the transition to the new change model (Brake, 2008; Kotter &Schlesinger, 2008). The volatility of the private sector ecosystems places different demands on managers relative to their public sector counterparts but is no less critical in terms of articulating change visions and obtaining commitment from followers (Alaa, 2009). Followers' commitment to the change initiative is not always grounded in a profound knowledge of the ideal objective facts or outcomes, but comes rather from interactions between people (Banutu-Gomez & Banutu-Gomez, 2007).

Literature Chronology

The public administration area, which includes federal, state, and local (e.g., county, city, or community) governmental agencies, has undergone significant change since 1980. During the intervening 30-year period, much of the attention has been on changes to the technical infrastructure to replace outdated applications and mainframes (Bellamy, 2010). The first 10-year phase began in the latter part of the 1970s and culminated with the passage of the first installment of the Paperwork Reduction Act (PRA), which was an attempt to interject efficient processes into governmental workflows (Koontz, 2005). The next 10-year phase included the remedial actions taken because of the Y2K problem that also exposed several technological weaknesses in governmental agencies' change initiative deployments, (Liou & Korosec, 2009; Radin, 1998).

The PRA requires chief information officers of federal agencies to review information collection activities and certify that those efforts meet performance standards to minimize administrative overhead and maximize the usefulness of the collected information (Bellamy, 2010; Koontz, 2006). The Paper Reduction Act established the Office of Management and Budget (OMB) as the oversight agency possessing the responsibility to provide guidance and adjudicate such data acquisitions and annual reporting relative to federal agencies' data collection burden (i.e., overheard) estimates (Koontz, 2006). In addition to the reporting responsibility, the PRA also indicates OMB personnel must provide best practices guidance in the form of administrative circulars to require adherence from monetary grant recipients and sub-recipients providing goods or services to the federal government (Steinhoff & Posner, 2010).

Because state and local governments are the largest recipients of federal funds, the effect of the circulars extends to most governmental operations. The federal government is also the largest purchaser of health care services through its Medicare and Medicaid programs, so the practical implications of the OMB circulars extends even further into the business and social environment of the United States (Letzring & Snow, 2011). The problems associated with the Y2K issue also became a major obstacle for the staff of agencies seeking to implement provisions of the PRA, the Government Performance and Results Act of 1993, and the Government Management and Results Act of 1994 (Jones & McCaffery, 2010; King & Cotterill, 2007).

Federal agency personnel had to upgrade most of their information systems because of the change from a hard coded two-digit date format to one that would accept four digits and provide the audit trails and security requirements set forth in the OMB circulars. Bellamy (2010) noted the unknown proposition of the dangers inherent in Y2K prompted governments in the United Kingdom and the United States to jettison carefully crafted risk assessment mechanisms and throw massive resources at the problem to eliminate, rather than just control the risk. The Y2K problems that never came to fruition should provide guidance regarding the management of pervasive, potentially large, yet unknowable risks, (e.g., global warming threats, energy or food insecurities, terrorism or pandemic diseases (Bellamy, 2010).

The information technology systems thought to be at risk from the Y2K date issue were innumerable and impacted massive data-processing systems (e.g., credit card transactions, hospital system, and air traffic control) that had been brought online over a period of decades (Sacheva, 2009). These systems were generally not interoperable and consisted of products from multiple vendors some of whom had gone out of business shortly after the product installation. Risk analysis under those conditions made estimating the lines of computer code that might suffer from the Y2K bug an insurmountable task (Posner, 2007).

Both the PRA and Y2K phases included a focus on technology, and opportunities that could have had meaningful workflow changes received a lower priority (Koontz, 2006). The Y2K phenomenon was an opportunity to review knowledge workflows and reengineer the work to take advantage of new technologies and collaboration tools (Barcan, 2009; Marsh, 2008). A review of the literature also revealed a third phase that indicated a slow shift from the traditional bureaucratic structure and its silo mentality to a post-bureaucratic organization design that has a flatter structure with permeable operational boundaries (Alan & Joanne, 2008; Ashkenas, et al, 2002; Grey & Garsten, 2001).

The shift from the bureaucratic structure to a post-bureaucratic design would seem to take advantage of more organic organizational structures that can respond rapidly to changes in the environment or in constituent needs and enhance citizen satisfaction in service delivery system (Butler & Allen, 2008; Jones, Jimmieson, & Griffiths, 2005). Taking full advantage of the paradigm shift requires an understanding of the progression of the shift as it relates to constituent preferences (Marsh, 2008). The change management direction relative to the development of service delivery structures is dependent on the effective use of information collection systems.

Information Resource Management in Government

The concept of information resource management (IRM) has a long history in the public administration sector of most developed countries (Bovaird, 2008; Butler & Allen, 2008; Gardner, 2009). IRM is not solely an issue in the governmental sector, as its tenets are also rooted in corporate and academic settings. Mettler 2007 noted the unique role of government directs agencies to manage information in a manner similar to how it manages other resources (e.g., personnel, money, and natural resources). Penn (1997) and Relyea (2000) posited that the ethereal composition of information, its inherent lack of intrinsic value, and its sustainability support the notion that management of information is an important organizational function.

The primary goal of the PRA is to provide assurance that in situations in which the government requests information from the public, the overhead burden associated with the production of that information is as minimal as possible and the information itself satisfies efficacy standards (Koontz, 2006). In practical terms this administrative simplification goal would direct agency personnel to gather information according to a set of standards (see Table 2) that ensure the minimization of the paperwork overhead on citizens while maximizing the value and usefulness of the collected information (Dawes, 2008).

The PRA provides authority to the OMB to establish standards and procedures (e.g., circulars and directives) for effective implementation and oversight of information collection (Koontz, 2005).

Another provision of the PRA requires agencies to obtain OMB approval of information collection procedures prior to their implementation. The 10th standard (see Table 2) appears to have the greatest propensity for change given the shrinkage of the technology life cycle and constituent communication preference (Bellamy, 2010). One constituent group prefers social media to communicate and transact business, whereas another group favors closer proximity of the transacting parties (e.g., service desks). Accommodating a comprehension level of service access for constituents requires options that include mobile communication and transaction processing (e.g., Facebook, Twitter, and LinkedIn) and also requires OMB approval. OMB gave that approval in April 2010 in the form of an exemption to the PRA content management provisions (e.g., record retention) and policies ("OMB Relaxes PRA Rules for Social Media," 2010).

The two primary components embedded in the concept of IRM are the laws and policies governing IRM and the conditions necessary for successful adoption (Caudie, 1988; Mischen, & Jackson, 2008; Sprehe, 1987). From a historical perspective, IRM became a prominent issue that led to the Brooks Act of 1965 and the legislating of formal controls in federal information technology resources (Ostroff, 2006). This initial legislative foray consisted of centralizing the purchase, leasing, maintenance, operation, and general use of technology into an agency charged with the review and authorization of those types of expenditures. Efforts to address the information component of IRM trace to the Federal Reports Act of 1942, which gave way to the PRA of 1980 (Caudle, 1988). The goal inherent in the passage of the PRA and its subsequent reauthorizations was a primary focus of relieving citizens of the burdens of information collection and reporting requirements to the federal government (Relyea, 2000).

Y2K remedial actions

The PRA of 1995 was another attempt to direct federal agencies to avail themselves of information technology innovations to avoid wasting billions of taxpayer dollars (Plocher, 1996). The genesis of the act was to require agency leadership to focus on program and process improvements that enhance operations. The reauthorization of PRA gave government officials "a systematic approach by which to manage related information resource activities and thereby improve government operations" (Plocher, 1996, p. 38). The 1995 PRA reenactment contained reform measures that interjected accountability and robust performance metrics and standards into the prevailing IRM conceptual template.

The impending challenges of Y2K led to a decrease in the importance of performance initiatives in order to address the perceived technology issues around the Y2K calendar event (Bellamy, 2010). Addressing the Y2K problem became the primary work effort for agencies so the performance improvement initiatives of PRA 1995 were delayed (Bellamy, 2010). In the interim, governmental agencies received notification that alignment of information management would be the primary focus, and subsequent mandates such as the Health Insurance Portability and Accountability Act (HIPAA) of 1996 and promulgation of several OMB circulars forced the issue to the forefront (Ford, 2008; Letzring & Snow, 2011).

With the emergence of the 1995 PRA Act, federal agencies encountered a growing chorus of legislative criticism for having out-of-date legacy systems of poor design, impending operating budget cutbacks, and pressures to downsize operations (Koontz, 2006). Given such a climate, agency leadership had to determine how to produce better outcomes from information technology investments. The intent of the PRA was to help federal agencies achieve the goal of improved outcomes by establishing requirements that such investments must align with programmatic management decisions and program performance (Plocher, 1996). In addition to cultural change that related to shifting a bureaucratic organization's operational mind-set and focus, responsiveness to citizens became more of a focus in agency leadership's tactical planning (Bovaird, 2008).

To facilitate a change in thinking, government leaders began to embrace complexity theory as a mechanism for transforming the organization into a more adaptive system (Arena, 2009). In most bureaucratic organizations, a shift to a more organic post-bureaucratic structure can represent a cultural change that at times resembles chaos (Robichau, 2011). The Health Insurance Portability and Accountability Act legislation was enacted under the mantle of administrative simplification because the health care industry had an inordinate number of electronic formats to submit transactions relating to health services provision to patients (Letzring & Snow, 2011). As the largest purchaser of health care services through the Medicare and Medicaid entitlement programs, the federal government saw an opportunity to change components of the delivery mechanism for these services (Jones & McCaffery, 2010). Health care was an appropriate choice for transaction simplification because the health care industry is emblematic of a complex system in which that the patient is the central component of the service provision of the various health care subsystems, (e.g., care-givers, laboratory, radiology, and finance).

In addition to requirements on health care providers seeking reimbursement for medical services, an opportunity existed to affect the information component is such a way that would transform the management of information through the deployment of standardized data practices and privacy requirements (Steinhoff & Posner, 2010). The Health Insurance Portability and Accountability Act changed the way managers interacted with the protected health care information that resided in the organization's computer systems and put the onus on them to manage that information in a stable computing environment (Ford, 2008). The pace of technology was chaotic and technology management was a moving target for business leaders (Hock, 1995; Karp & Helgø, 2008; Kira & Van Eijnatten, 2008). This environmental uncertainty gave chaordic leadership its foothold in corporate enterprises.

Chaordic leadership describes a self-managing, adaptive, nonlinear, and complex system, whether that system is biological, physical, or social; the characteristic predispositions of which manifests states of order and chaos or, resembling business terminology relating to cooperation and competition (Hock, 1995). Chaos theory is a hallmark of complex adaptive systems because of the complexity of the actors in the fitness landscape (Carlisle & McMillan, 2006; Karp & Helgø, 2008). The fitness landscape describes the space within which agents of a complex system react to environmental disruptions by ascending to adjacent fitness peaks.

Fitness peaks represent dimensions within a landscape map that maximizes the collective benefits that accrue to of the members of the social system (Mischen & Jackson, 2008). Achieving these peaks presents multiple relationship behavior possibilities available to landscape actors through the contextualized perspectives and actions of the individual actors inhibiting the landscape (Ailon, 2008; Teisman & Klijn, 2008). Teisman and Klijn (2008) noted that such a landscape is a space in which humans exist, interact, and continuously react to environmental disruptions as a result of individual decisions of land-scape agents, internal or external pressures, and the determination of the effectiveness of the agents' survival behavior (e.g., short- versus long-term gains).

Ailon (2008) also endorsed this adaptive concept and noted that within cultural dimensions there exists a contextual sense that presents in a state of affairs behind which any number of alternate presentations exists. David Hume advanced a similar viewpoint relative to the dimensions of culture and the interactions inherent in relationships inhibiting the landscape as driven by cultural belief structures inherent to a particular group. An understanding of how cultural groups develop intentional beliefs relative to unobserved causation beliefs (e.g., origin of the universe), beliefs about enduring objects (e.g., religious symbols), and how these beliefs can influence thoughts, ancillary beliefs, passions, and resultant behavior or actions (Marusis, 2010).

Cultural relativism perspectives have a prominent role in any assessment of the environmental conditions and stimuli that interact with actors in the fitness landscape (Millican, 2009; Scherbaum & Dshemuchadse, 2008). From an organizational perspective, the actions of a workforce result from the discourse that binds the group as a collective (Ailon, 2008; Foxon, Reed, & Stringer, 2009). An organizational discourse also brings the prospect of knowledge engineering as a predictor or indicator of how interactions between the various actors occur and the effect of relationship outcomes within and outside of the organizational boundaries (Robert, Dennis, & Hung, 2009). A multidisciplinary approach for enhancing enterprise outcomes and organizational learning supports maximizing knowledge, which includes the review, design, and implementation of social and technological events and process flows that enhance the creation, sharing, and application of knowledge (deLeon & Varda, 2009; Symon, 2000).

Knowledge engineering is a primary concern in developing innovative and knowledge sharing behaviors that facilitate the management of "complexity and ambiguity using knowledge networks and connections, exploring smart processes, and deploying people-centric technologies" (Crawford, et al, 2009, p. 6). Such an approach serves as the foundation for the deployment of enterprise resource planning applications that take a somewhat bureaucratic approach to managing explicit knowledge and process workflows that are algorithmic or linear in orientation (Dovifat, Brtiggemeier, & Lenk, 2007; Ifinedo & Nahar, 2007). Supplementing ERP applications are knowledge bases that contain collaboration tools that allow knowledge workers to share tacit knowledge or more of the experience based type of knowledge that resides in a worker's brain (Ifinedo & Nahar, 2007; Lowe & Locke, 2008). This knowledge management approach is the new genesis of current change management initiatives, (Nan, 2011).

The Post-bureaucratic transformation

The review of literature revealed that a line exists in the theory and design between bureaucratic and post-bureaucratic organizations. The distinction is drawn along mechanistic characteristics incumbent in bureaucracies compared to the more organic features inherent in post-bureaucratic organizations (Alaa, 2009). Classic management theory indicates the bureaucratic design is the whole consisting of the sum of its subsystems or functions (Rethemeyer, 2009).

In the classic management scenario, the role of managers is to plan work activities and monitor workers' performance to ensure adherence to organizational policies and procedures (Steinhoff & Posner, 2010; Rethemeyer, 2009). The expectation is that workers will behave like replaceable components in the organizational mechanism (Calderón-Ruiz & Sepúlveda, 2011). Bureaucratic organizations have a central authority that occupies a position in a hierarchical structure that emphasizes a unity of command, division of work, and predictable conforming behaviors. Nonconformity results in punitive forms of punishment, which hampers meaningful communication and feedback (Pollitt, 2009).

In some cases, these bureaucratic systems can produce distorted data presentations because management will receive only favorable information (Gilley, McMillan, & Gilley, 2009). In other cases, post-bureaucratic theory posits a team-oriented organizational design spatially and temporally flexible and less rigid than its bureaucratic counterpart (Ford, 2008). Cross-functional teams also embrace the permeability of organizational barriers (silos) to increase horizontal management (Ashkenas et al, 2002); Boyd, 2009). Innovations in information technology create opportunities for omni-directional networks and feedback mechanisms that replace traditional top-down bureaucratic communication flows (Agin & Gibson, 2010). No undisputable definition exists for a post-bureaucratic organization, but its primary characteristic is its complex adaptive system orientation (Alaa, 2009).

The goal of a post-bureaucratic enterprise is to engage knowledge workers at every organizational level to contribute to the decision-making process, share information, and collaborate in any solution-finding effort (deLeon & Varda, 2009; Grey & Garsten, 2001). A situation in contrast with bureaucratically controlled entities that dictate global solutions and implement those decisions using a top-down implementation strategy (Haynes, 2008). For those organizations that exist in stable or less volatile market situations, a mechanistic bureaucratic organizational form may be a good fit (Jun, 2009). Hierarchical structures with clearly defined roles and lines of authority may provide the predictable results needed in that environment.

If the operating environment is not stable or a high degree of volatility and competition exists, a more organic organizational form may be more suitable (Foxon et al, 2009). Such systems have informal and more open lines of authority and communication as well as a diverse decision-making mechanism (Ford, 2008). Such enterprises interact with other actors in their ecosystem and can react to environmental uncertainty by self-organizing resources to counteract environmental turbulence.

Possessing this self-organizing ability is critical for the management of the innovation process and also positions the leaders of an organization to be successful in their succession planning relating to the generational workforce because enterprise resources are active in problem-solving activities (Graetz & Smith, 2009). Developing an organizational culture that embraces innovation requires leadership that focuses more on transformative behaviors and less on the transactional management components (Jamrog, Vickers, & Bear, 2006). Tantamount to developing an innovative culture is leadership that demonstrates respect, creates transparency, ensures equity, clarifies expectations, practices accountability, and keeps promises (Hovenga, Kidd, Garde, & Hullin Lucay Cossio, 2010).

A primary function of transformational leadership is to foster, develop, and nurture intimacy. Enhancing quality of work life and disciplined unselfishness only develops through the establishment of close social relationships (Gumusluoğlu & Ilsev, 2009). A high level of empathy is important because it demonstrates that leaders care about employees and a trusting relationship forms between leaders and employees (Hornung, Rousseau, & Glaser, 2008). Such a relationship creates a transactional trust relationship that can survive the bumps in the road that occur in organizations in the face of turmoil (Brake, 2008).

Trust is a key element attributable to effective transformational leadership. Broken trust can result in adverse effects on a worker's performance (Brake, 2008; Grey & Garsten, 2001). Leaders must diligently work to establish relationship-based trust in the change process, which occurs by the creation of a positive workplace environment that promotes emotional connection amongst employees (Hornung, Rousseau, & Glaser, 2008; Jamrog et al, 2006). Such a scenario reinforces the need for a robust organizational team-building effort that stresses the development of transactional trust between organizational team members (Brake, 2008; Krane, 2008).

Graetz and Smith (2009) noted that organizations operating in a consistent or predictable environment using standard technology tools would operationally function at a high level. However, if that organization inhibits a space in more turbulent and uncertain environments, superior level of performance would benefit from a more flexible and organic approach. A representative glimpse of such a future might be seen in the current case study of the county local government structure that is undertaking substantial organizational changes (e.g., enterprise resource planning implementation, a results-only workplace environment, and horizontal management).

These organizational change initiatives take advantage of technology and resemble a complex adaptive system (Valerdi, Nightingale, & Blackburn, 2009). Such systems consist of actors (entities or social groups), individuals, and groups that echo emphatically through the sharing of commonalties relating to societal norms, knowledge bases, or goals attributable to its cultural propensities of interaction and perspective sharing (Van Mierlo, Rutte, Vermunt, Kompier, & Doorewaard, 2007). Actors respond to external stimuli (e.g., from its ecosystem, other complex adaptive systems, or actors) and internal pressures emanating from the actors' encounters with interdependency and conflict constraints when the need conflicts occur between actors (Arena, 2009; Aydinoglu, 2010; Bovaird, 2008), some of which can be seen in a need to control an information distribution process versus a more open process that provides access to more information.

According to Dawes (2008), Dovifat, Brüggemeier, and Lenk (2007), and Sacheva (2009), the migration to e-governance has policy framework objectives that interrelate in terms of government processes and constituent interactions. A policy framework relates to the rules and conditions for the collection, storage, use, and protection of information. Enhanced public services that provide affordances that have a customer-facing orientation and access convenience for constituents and business partners seeking programmatic information regarding services available from governmental agencies (Persson & Goldkuhl, 2010; Yeo, 2009).

The provision of high-quality and cost-efficient government operations requires the implementation of improvement projects that focus on efficiency, infrastructure enhancements, information management, and the use of the information resource (Wagenaar, 2007). Citizen engagement in democratic processes should include accessible and usable technologies, transparent information content, constituent interactions, public conversations on political issues, and public collaboration or a process that engages citizens in the agenda-setting process (Dawes, 2008). This interactive future includes administrative reforms that have a firm basis in operational concepts relating to accountability, transparency, and trust. The trend throughout the 1990s and early 2000s has been to emphasize reforms in public management and the literature dates back to the PRAs of the 1980s. The goal of these outcome improvement initiatives was to improve management efficiency, control, coordination, leadership, and operational performance, which many believe are important functional objectives for fostering effective government (Relyea, 2000).

Such reforms largely pertain to the organizational structure and workflow processes of government in addition to the role and function of government representatives to the private and not-for profit industry segments that carry out public functions. The reforms must also include changing the organizational culture of government agencies and the manner in which the public service workforce perceive its role relative to governance, constituents, and general society (Robichau, 2011). The challenge of e-government extends beyond effective information technology management, enterprise-wide adaptation, and technical competence and serves as a foundation for governmental discourse (Dawes, 2008).

President Barack Obama made the following announcement in his 2009 Inaugural address:

"Those of us who manage the public's dollars will be held to account—to spend wisely, reform bad habits and do our business the right way— because only then can we restore the vital trust between a people and their government."

The next day, the president announced guiding doctrines for his administration: that government should be transparent, participatory, and collaborative, (Steinhoff & Posner, 2010). Accomplishing such a goal requires an organizational cultural change to the concept of governance such that value-add service provision become possible (Osborne & Gaebler, 1992). Sacheva (2009) noted the probability of success in organizational change is a product of several interactive factors.

Sacheva (2006) presented the factors in the form of an equation $D \times V \times P > R$, where D is equal to dissatisfaction with the current state, V equals a possible future vision, P represents the probability of resources available to meet the vision, and R equals resistance. The practical application of this formula posits that "if D, V, or P is absent or low, then the product will be low and therefore not capable of overcoming the resistance" (Sacheva, 2009, p. 113). Resistance can also represent a cost of change in terms of economic and psychological factors (Walker, 2005). Leaders of post-bureaucratic organizations must weigh a series of complex variables to effect change in a sustainable manner and consistent with their environment (Yoon & Kuchinke, 2005).

Change leadership represents sets of behaviors that serve to mitigate the adverse consequences complex organizational variables can have on a change initiative. Lyons, Swindler, and Offner (2009) noted the behaviors overlap with transformational leadership concepts and qualities such as visioning, creating urgency, and commitment to the change. Change leadership represents specific and episodic characteristics that address imminent change events, in contrast to transformational leadership style that represents stability over time (Graml, Bracht, & Spies, 2008). The overlap might manifest in a situation in which functional transformative leaders deploy cultural change leadership devices as part of exerting their influence on organizations. Prior research has shown that these leadership styles can work synergistically and produce effects on employee behavior outcomes (Lyons et al, 2009).

Exercising change leadership tactics includes developing work environments that embrace and promote a culture of results orientation. Such a culture transforms the workforce that becomes customer-focused, collaborative, and knowledge centric that fosters innovative change creation (Neves, 2009). Transformational leaders provide the linkage between individual performance and organizational success (Mihm, 2007). A core component in maintaining the linkage is the presence of a mechanism for measuring agency performance. Such systems are not simply appropriate for periodic individual goal achievement and ratings processes, but as tools to facilitate the daily management of the enterprise (Sutanto, Kankanhalli, Raman, & Tan, 2008). These systems promote the achievement of operational outcomes, accelerate the pace of change, and facilitate bi-directional communication throughout the business cycle so that discussions concerning individual and organizational performance are congruent and continuous (Mihm, 2007).

The composite of transformational change represents a departure from a state of organic internal change to policy-focused change that originates in intersecting organizational discourses (Boden, Cox, & Nedeva, 2006). The first discourse relates to an epistemological transference in the normal science paradigm, the second consists of neoliberal perspective of science and its contribution to economic sustainability and knowledge management, and third is that states are too large and inefficient in their resource transformation (Boden et al, 2006). The existing literature provides an overview of the complex components inherent in change initiatives and the interconnectedness of those components. The following section indicates practical applications of the change management process and includes mechanisms that can serve as predictors of success in change initiatives.

Synthesis of Recent Literature

The focus of much of the recent literature is on technical components of government workflows while giving very little attention to the cultural aspects that workers contribute to the work of the agency (Barcan, 2009; Dawes, 2008; Jones & McCaffery, 2010; Liou & Korosec, 2009; Powner, 2004). The literature is also complete in terms of its change management coverage, and the complex issues that inhibit the successful completion of change initiatives in the manner management envisions at its inception. The literature is lacking in the application of complexity theory to the planning and execution of organizational changes that have a broad effect on knowledge workers and the population that these workers serve or to which they provide programmatic services.

The decision making by knowledge workers relative to organizational goal follows a nonlinear, continuous, and self-organizing principle of cognition (Mischen & Jackson, 2008). Self-organizational cognition studies include the fields of macro and microeconomics, psychology, and neuroscience. The literature is not replete with studies of leadership behavior from a complexity theory approach to explain the acceptance or rejection of organization change initiatives. Complexity theory is a well-researched topic experiencing resurgence in its application to organizational structures (Alaa, 2009; Haynes, 2008; Arena, 2009; Valerdi et al, 2009).

The resurgence of this theory is attributable to the complexity that exists in the relationships of an organization as its leadership executes its resource transformation process. The nonlinearity of those relationships requires the organizational leaders to adopt a complex adaptive system approach to enhance organizational performance and ensure its survival (Krane, 2008). This complex adaptive system mind-set is prevalent in the private sector economy, but it also can be found in the public administration arena. According to Ostroff (2006), leaders of private sector organizations achieve substantial productivity gains by deploying strategies to uncover marketplace solutions to social needs, but high-performing government agencies can resemble well-managed enterprises.

This private sector resemblance can be found in a review of an organization's mission statement, goals and objectives, rational process design, accountability, and the effectiveness of its leaders (Carlisle & McMillan, 2006; Gardner, 2009). These private and public organizations differ in terms of purpose, organizational culture, and operational context, (e.g., profit versus nonprofit orientation). These differences are significant because government serves a unique role in society and its operation by design is to serve the greater number of its members as opposed to being a profit seeking-organization with more parochial concerns (e.g., customer base).

The application of a complex adaptive system approach would seem appropriate because of the volatility that exists in relationships of the agents (e.g., people, organizations, groups) that inhibit a fitness landscape. This book will involve an attempt to bridge the gaps in the literature between the motivated and rational self-interest of landscape actors and the global concerns of the shared ecosystem, relative to long and short-term personal goals. To define the conditions that allow workers to share and collaborate in the achievement efforts of organizational objectives and goals requires articulation and reconciliation of worker's personal goals (Hornung et al, 2008; Spangenburg, 2014).

Ifinedo and Nahar (2007) described six dimensions that can serve as predictors of a successful organizational initiative which included on two quality and four impact factors. The quality factors are systemic (information and system), which, when taken in concert with the soft and hard skill impact factors (individual, organizational, vendor/consultant, and workgroup), can determine the level of success in an initiative. Newman (2006) noted the failure of enterprise initiatives can be attributed more to flaws in the organizational engagement strategy than to the technical solution. Other factors that influence the success or failure of an enterprise initiative can include "inadequate support from key leaders, inadequate buy-in from those affected, confusion about results and accountabilities, slow reaction to roadblocks, continued allegiance to old processes and behavior" (Newman, 2006, p. 84).

In a practical construct, enterprise-wide initiatives must identify as many organizational moving parts as possible and develop mitigation strategies to enhance the probability of success (Barcan, 2009). The goal of these initiative efforts is to determine whether the development and deployment of alternative technology solutions can achieve desirable and predictable outcomes (Janson & Scheiner, 2007). These efforts require attention to the process of change itself and a determination of the ability of organizational leaders to effect change (Jones, Jimmieson, & Griffiths, 2005). Many organizational leaders use a change effectiveness equation to measure the ability of an enterprise to implement the change in its workflow processes successfully (Bovaird, 2008).

This equation $Q \times A = E$ provides a relatively straight forward way to describe the change phenomenon (Newman, 2006). In the equation, the effectiveness (E) of a change effort is equal to the quality (Q) of the strategy and the acceptance (A) intensity of that strategy. Many entities have chosen to implement change projects using the change acceleration process (CAP) model developed by General Electric (Von Der Linn, 2009). The change acceleration process (CAP) model process has seven layers and a set of tools that allows team to implement and lead change initiatives (Newman, 2006; Polk, 2011).

Von Der Linn, (2009) advanced a model for implementing and accelerating the organizational change process. The CAP model focuses on the management and work team behavioral aspects of change as competitive implementation advantages, and less on the technical component or competency (Polk, 2011). Newman (2006) noted that competitive advantage and the resulting profitability emerges from the implementation of complex change in a laser focused manner, which requires devoting time and resources in addition to a strategic change decision. Critical elements inherent in the CAP model relate to leading change, fostering a shared need, vision shaping, mobilizing commitment, change permanency, process monitoring, and modifying existing systems and structures.

Leading change: Leaders of committed organizations must exercise leadership for the life of the change initiative and this commitment is vital to the success of the initiative. A project management perspective bears a significant risk of failure if there is lack of leadership commitment.

Creating a shared need: The need for the proposed change must outweigh its internal resistance and organizational propensity to maintain the status quo. Compelling change rationale must resonate with every organizational level.

Shaping a vision: Organizational leaders must advance a clear and attainable vision of a future state that relates to current operational reality. Leaders must articulate and clearly describe what the future will resemble at the conclusion. A journey that does not have a clear and visible destination or outcome is much the same as wandering. Clarity and acceptance are not always mutually inclusive terms.

Mobilizing commitment: At the point of achieving leadership support, compelling change logic, a clear vision of the future and the ingredients necessary for rolling out the initiative, the next task is building an influence strategy to foster momentum. Making change last: Layers 2-4 involve accelerating the change adoption, whereas Layers 5-7 concern the task of change permanency. Leveraging process wins and applying the knowledge gained from pilot projects to the broader rollout.

Monitoring process: It is important to plan for the measurement process to assess the progress of the change. Benchmarks must be set and an assessment made of how well they are met. Performance metrics assist in the monitoring process and provide the appropriate improvement targets.

Changing systems and structures: The organizational subsystems (e.g., human resources, information technology systems, and resource allocation) generally support the current state of the enterprise operations. Alterations to these systems are necessary to support the future state of business operations in order to circumvent the tendency to revert to past practices. The CAP model provides a framework for management to successfully develop, manage, and monitor change initiatives to successful conclusion.

Conclusions

The literature reviewed included complex adaptive system and complexity theory application because of the idiosyncratic behavior of social service systems and the service delivery organizational structures that respond in the nonlinear manner inherent to their particular fitness landscape. This selection criterion was appropriate because the relationships that emerge during the self-organization process are dynamic and occur in an organic bottom-up fashion that defies measurement and prediction using quantitative methods. Such methods seek a causal relationship not inherent to the qualitative composition of complex adaptive systems. The focus of a phenomenological study is the experiences of participants and the responses that occur to stimuli in a fitness landscape (Mahoney, 2010; Teisman & Klijn, 2008; Yin, 2009).

These landscape stimuli events cause the individual actors to self-organize and develop appropriate responses to destabilizing factors to regain balance (Teisman & Klijn, 2008). The balance can represent conditions of satisfaction in a social network or ecosystem (Carlisle & McMillan, 2006). An example could be constituent satisfaction with the status quo for communication with public officials using conventional means such as a telephone. If technology provides a more interactive medium such as a website or blog, it can upset the status quo until communication equilibrium is brought back into balance.

Technology is the best example of a disturbing event that cause disequilibrium in an ecosystem, and one has only to look at mobile technology to find examples of the effect Yeo, 2009). It is therefore appropriate to include complex interactive systems in the response mechanism for designing policy and program change initiatives. Future research should include studying the role of computer modeling and artificial intelligence software in providing leaders with additional tools that have predictive value (Amblard, 2007).

The tools could allow leaders to simulate a variety of operational scenarios that account for the nonlinear relationship interactions that occur in social settings. Using computer modeling, organizational leaders could construct fitness landscapes that include agents (e.g., people, technology, or entities) and manipulate each variable, observe the effects, and formulate strategies based on the range of possible outcomes the fitness landscape exercise produces. The fitness landscape exercises could also include action research and soft system methodology to validate outcome generation (Yan & Yan, 2010).

This soft system research direction aligns with the construct that organizational work settings are sociotechnical systems that generate services or products by design (Yan, 2007). The collective actions of agents in these sociotechnical systems interact in nonlinear patterns most appropriate for study using complexity theory methods and chaordic system thinking approaches (Kira & Van Eijnatten, 2008). The approaches contextualize organizations as ecosystems that achieve levels of sustainability by deploying diverse resource to adapt to external forces.

To accomplish this contextualization and resulting sustainability requires the creation of a holon system that also allows its agents to mature in its internalization of interior and exterior complexities (Kira & Van Eijnatten, 2008). The complexity of organizational environments would seem to dictate an approach that allows every member of the organizations to maximize participation in the resource transformation process and effectively respond to constituent or market demands. The focus of the current research will be identifying the essential leadership components necessary to develop and deploy the type of organizational culture that allows productive and predictive workflows. These components include an ability to adapt leadership styles appropriate to the cultural environment and the emotional intelligence to develop and maintain relationships based on transactional trust (Brake, 2008; Liu, Siu, & Shi, 2010; Robert, Dennis, & Hung, 2009).

Summary

Recent developments in complex adaptive systems point to the use of artificial intelligence applications to provide evolutionary agent responses to various shifts in its environmental equilibrium (Desouza &, 2011), which would allow the deployment of computer applications that could simulate environmental variables in a fitness landscape to obtain a predictive response to various disruptions (e.g., decreased resources, citizen response, or technology innovations). Future organizational leaders must have tools that allow enterprises to understand and anticipate the operational environment and formulate innovative strategies to deliver the goods and services its constituents or customers demand, and do so in the time and space convenient to them (Gumusluoğlu & Ilsev, 2009; Xu et al, 2007).

Leaders must also possess a keen understanding of their organizational culture so that all components of the workforce can work collectively to formulate a response in the best interest of the organizational ecosystem (Bloch, 2005; Boden et al, 2006; Gang, Shu-tao, & Qiang, 2009). The Chinese referred to this latter condition as quanxi, which Wong (2010) noted is the societal norm for human interactions and as such resembles a complex adaptive system. Quanxi is not confined to personal interactions but can also serve as an operational basis for social networks to provide organizational congruency.

The practical application of this quanxi phenomenon is a clear preference for cooperative work efforts, participative decisions, and strong emergent relationships to ensure group effectiveness (Wong, 2010). An organizational mindset that focuses on the collective well-being of the system would allow the enterprise to be flexible in its market space and maintain a strong leader-to-follower relationship. Chapter 3 contains a discussion on the methodology chosen to provide insight into those conditions that allow the creation of an organizational culture that promotes and sustains relationship transparency, transactional trust, knowledge sharing, collaboration, and innovative problem solving.

CHAPTER 3

Research Methodologies deployed in original study

The qualitative study's purpose was to examine the cultural and operational (e.g., leadership) composition of the various programmatic actors (e.g., knowledge workers, residents, community partners, and community stakeholders) engaged in the delivery of innovative social and program services to the residents of the county. An examination included the operational effect of the relationships between these actors and how they precipitate the preferred design configuration for the delivery mechanism for social or public services. A qualitative method is appropriate because such studies deploy flexible designs and subjective methods with smaller samples of participants in an effort to produce tentative new insights, deeper understandings, and theoretically enriched observations (Rubin, 2008). Additionally, the results of the study will provide an understanding of how each actor's cultural and value dimension perspectives follow a complexity theory model to assess the nonlinear effect that environmental changes in the social ecosystem has on an actor fitness landscape situation and how it serves as the foundation for subsystem self-organization to achieve desired outcomes. The figure below illustrates a logical model to articulate the nonlinear effects that contribute to the production of innovative change in social program construction.

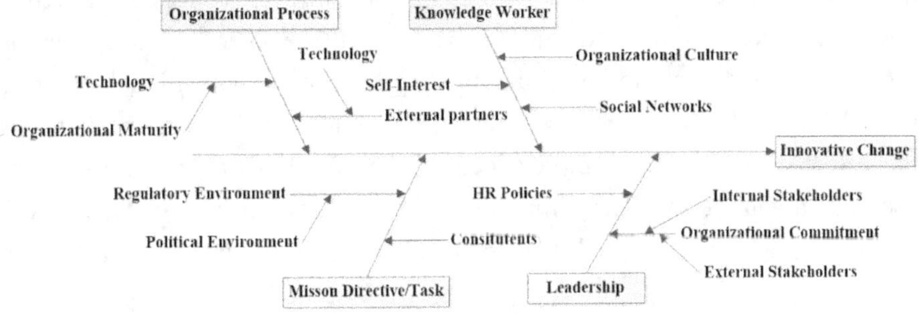

Nonlinear effects to the production of innovative change

A descriptive case study research design was conducted to study subjective (e.g., emotional relationship orientation) and objective (e.g., competence and integrity) behaviors models that emerge during the process of organizational change as well as leadership behaviors found in state and local government agencies where change initiatives occur. The descriptive theory this design encompasses is that leadership behavior patterns relative to change events are the greater predictors of success or failure, and transformational leadership qualities are essential to creating a culture of collaboration, cooperation, knowledge sharing, and innovation (Jones, Jimmieson, & Griffiths, 2005; Liu, Siu, O., & Shi, 2010). The behavioral patterns are thought to be critical to articulating the organizational vision eliciting follower acceptance of the vision aligning internal, external, and individual objectives modeling a desirable code of conduct and establishing transactional trust (Brake, 2008).

The variability that exists in complex systems can produce unreliable outcomes in a quantitative research method. Such a method seeks to uncover strict causal relationships not readily found in complex adaptive system relationships and self-organizing behavior patterns (Gumusluoğlu & Ilsev, 2009; Schwandt, 2007). The case study design will assist in the isolation of conditions that contribute to self-organization in the system and the relationship structures that emerge.

The case study research design was appropriate because of the complexity that exists in each actor's response mechanism and experience in the fitness landscape and the complex interactions that occur between those actors during the service delivery process (Chorba, 2011; Mahoney, 2010; Teisman & Klijn, 2008). The design of this book aligns well with the problem-solving dilemma inherent in the determination of the most appropriate organizational structure and culture that allows the formation of cost-effective delivery mechanisms that effectively meets the complex needs of citizens. Use of complexity theory provided a vehicle for determining the extent and composition of those needs as well as the organizational workforce relationships incumbent in those objectives.

The topic of this book included a complex adaptive system approach that includes a number of interrelated environmental components and the motivated self-interest behaviors that need acknowledgment and reconciliation during organizational change initiatives (e.g., change and process management).

Mischen and Jackson (2008) noted that the emergence of such behaviors can determine the success or failure of change initiatives because they define the linkage between interrelated knowledge management concepts, social network analysis, and complexity theory and application of those concepts to the examination of intra and inter-organizational policy development and deployment. Connecting these conceptual components assists in the development and deployment of the organizational response to challenges to its operational ecosystem. The research questions design seeks to establish and identify the leadership behavior patterns that produce desirable workflow outcomes.

Population

The general population group for this book was the management knowledge workers who perform duties for the largest county in Minnesota, which number approximately 1500 of the total county workforce. The target population included approximately 1200 staff from upper, middle, and line management groups who have experienced change initiatives in recent months and possess at least 5 years of work experience with the county. Employees with 10 years or more experience (i.e., 720 staff members) will be sought for individual interviews because this group would likely have longitudinal experience spanning organizational initiatives such as process or procedure modifications, staff realignments, department reorganizations, and new role assignments (Gilley, McMillan, & Gilley, 2009; Jamrog, Vickers, & Bear, 2006; Neves, 2009; Schwandt, 2007).

Employees with at least 10 years of tenure will have more familiarity with the county's operations because of their interactions with at least three different county administrations, which might indicate significant change acceptance tendencies. This book's population also best represented the county's change readiness based on its cultural maturity level which can determine the effectiveness of organizational leadership visions and the responsiveness of staff to those changes (e.g., developmental, transitional, or transformational). Developmental change refers to the reconfiguration of prevailing structures and processes, transitional change implies new process introduction or technology, and transformational change involves the emergence of a new operational paradigm (Long & Spurlock, 2008). The type of change initiative has a direct bearing on decision making relative to the most appropriate implementation strategy.

Study participation

This book involved deployment of nonprobability convenience sampling of the county's knowledge worker management hierarchy (i.e., upper, middle, and line staff levels). The purposive sample of 21 study subjects (i.e., seven participants per level) consisted of four staff members in each of three focus group meetings and nine individual staff interviews equally distributed to each management stratum (Bhattacherjee, 2012; Rubin, 2008; Willis, 2007). Obtaining a smaller number of focus group participants provided sufficient opportunity for staff to be heard and to express their opinions in a nonthreatening setting (Neuman, 2005; Schwandt, 2007; Yin, 2009). Characteristics of the focus group participants included a cross-section of staff that displayed generational, ethnic, and gender diversity with more than five years of employment with the county. The current case study also included a selection of knowledge workers from the executive branch of the county to include appointed and elected officials, (i.e., commissioners and administrators). Middle management knowledge workers consisted of area directors, area managers, and program managers.

Line staff supervisors completed the sample. The purposeful sampling selection criteria for participants also included generation, tenure, educational and technical background, employment diversity, and supervisory background components. The intent of this sampling method was to ensure that a sufficient cross-section of knowledge workers provide a base of experience and operational viewpoints. Employees chosen for staff interviews displayed similar characteristics but additionally had a county employment history that exceeds 10 years. Employees with at least 10 years of tenure will have more familiarity with the county's operations because of their interactions with at three different county administrations, which would demonstrate significant change acceptance tendencies.

Data Collection Procedures

The study deployment involved conducting three focus groups consisting of four the county staff in each grouping (e.g., upper, middle, and lower management levels) who receive similar instructions and questions. Data was collected from 21 purposively selected county supervisory knowledge workers possessing five or more years of continuous employment with the county using a combination of focus group meetings, focused interviews, and direct observations. Data collection occurred in onsite facilities at the county's main office in downtown Minneapolis, Minnesota. However, the interviews were flexible in scheduling to accommodate individual participant availability or preference.

Participant consent was also sought for digitally recording of focus group and focused interviews to ensure the most accurate record of the proceedings and transcribed by an external transcription service provider (Schwandt, 2007; Yin, 2009).

Direct observations occurred over a four-month period and involved researcher participation in strategic and operational events or meetings that embodied the research questions and case study focus as approved by project sponsors (i.e., county management personnel). Approved research projects at the county must have one or more upper management sponsors to assist in the resource procurement process and provide access to relevant organizational settings (e.g., retreats, planning sessions, and strategy development). Some advantages of direct observations are that this source of evidence provides situational and contextual realities to the case study. Another advantage is the interpersonal insight that can be gained by observation of participants' behavior and potential follower motivations for change acceptance (Neuman, 2005; Rubin, 2008).

Three focus group meetings were conducted over a nine-week period with each meeting occurring in three-week intervals that were sensitive to participants' schedules. Participants selected for these focus group meetings possessed county employment histories greater than five years. The meetings occurred in conference rooms at the county Government Center in downtown Minneapolis. Nine focused interviews were conducted in the offices of the selected participants or an alternate setting if desired by a participant (e.g., a conference room). Participants selected for focused interviews possessed county employment histories of greater than 10 years to ensure a base of comparing intervening county administrations.

The logic of this sample size was reflective of the relevance each participant has to the research questions and change leadership concepts under study as opposed to representativeness to the study population (Neuman, 2005; Schwandt, 2007; Yin, 2009). The selection criteria for participants in the sample were direct supervisory responsibilities, five or more years of continuous county employment, and involvement in one or more change related events (e.g., department reorganization or technology implementation). The relevance each participant displays was his or her perspective of the organizational decision-making and leadership behaviors relative to change initiatives.

The chosen sample size embodied a representational mapping of the organizational structure that reflects a schema of the temporal, ritual, and routine features of the people, organizations, or social interactions under observation (Schwandt, 2007). Data collection from the focus group included digital recordings and meeting note transcriptions. Interview data collection proceeded according to a structured interview question format.

A pilot focus group consisted of a cross section of county staff to validate the focus group questions prior to conducting the larger group meetings. To obtain corroboration of the data, it was triangulated with information obtained through focus group meetings, structured interviews, and participant-observations to ensure a convergence of the evidence of the role leadership has in fostering innovative change (Rubin, 2008; Yin, 2009). The format of the case study report is in a linear-analytic structure in that the topical materials was sequential and begin with the problem statement, review of relevant literature, research methods, data collection findings and analysis, and conclusions and implications (Yin, 2009). The report also included a review of current organizational processes, practices, and operation as well as the desired organizational model. The data collection instruments were thought to be the most appropriate method of obtaining the experiences of workers because the format allows reflective answers rather than standard agree or disagree-type responses.

The following paragraphs present an overview of the current single case study's research questions. The context of this book was partial fulfillment of the requirements for a doctorate in management degree and its focus was on determining the leadership factors essential for success in change initiatives precipitating from environmental events (e.g., budget shortfalls, constituent demands, political interventions, and regulatory constraints). The perspective of the study was from that of organizational knowledge workers who inhibit the fitness landscape of the county, and the complex interrelationship and interactions that occur as disruptive events force the system from equilibrium. The four general topic areas that the case study focus group and individual interview participants addressed were as follows:

Define the organizational culture here at the county and what are the key components inherent in change opportunities?

What are key leadership components you feel are necessary to promote innovation change (e.g., workflow collaboration, cooperation, and knowledge sharing)?

Responsive government: What does the term mean relative to operational change as it relates to mobilizing organizational resources to achieve that change?

What is the appropriate role for external partners or communities of interest in the operation and structure of governmental agency workflows?

Substantial discourse occurred as each topic area was explored. Each topic area contained 15-20 minutes of digital recordings that were part of the study protocols. A parking lot recording format was deployed to collect ideas or themes unrelated to the topic area, but were thought by the group to need further articulation, notation, or discussion in a separate venue.

Validity and Reliability

The quality control measures deployed in this book to ensure validity (i.e., construct, internal, and external) and ensure reliability included data collection and triangulation from multiple information sources (i.e., focus groups, interviews, and direct observations). Reliability measures included the county management review, pattern matching, theory building, and analytic generalization (Baxter & Jack, 2008; Chorba, 2011; Mahoney, 2010; Yin, 2009). These measures were critical to ensuring that the true and certain findings of social science research accurately represent the essences of the phenomena to which they refer, and backed by empirical data (Schwandt, 2007). To obtain corroboration of the data, it was triangulated with information obtained through the three focus group meetings, nine structured interviews, and participant-observations to ensure a convergence of the evidence of the role leadership has in fostering innovative change (Rubin, 2008; Yin, 2009). Data collection from participants was analyzed and triangulated to ensure that the chain of evidence follows from the case study questions through to the report conclusions (Chorba, 2011; Prince, Manolis, & Tratner, 2009; Yin, 2009).

Data Analysis

According to Neuman, (2005) data analysis comprises examination, categorization, tabulation, testing, or recombining evidentiary material to arrive at empirically based conclusion. Documents from the focus group, individual interviews, and organization artifacts (e.g., project plans, governance directives, or meeting agendas) were compiled and analyzed using NVivo 10 software to develop data themes, patterns, and correlations. Coding of the data followed previously identified patterns that the researcher expects to emerge during the focus group interactions and preferences of interview participants.

Assumptions or Expected Findings

The expectation of the study was that transformational leadership is the most significant factor in the determination of success in the implementation of cultural change initiatives. Transformational leadership behavior emerged as a critical factor in the deployment of an organizational culture that values knowledge creation, collaboration, and innovation. An ancillary outcome of the study might also be a communication template for introducing cultural change initiatives to internal and external audiences.

Summary

Previous research on leadership behavior patterns advances the theory that the development of innovative cultures is dependent on how well organizational leaders understand the dimensional aspects of the prevailing culture, particularly which dimensions are local and which are global in construct. An important consideration for leaders is to take note of and recognize the differences in the inherent value structure relative to the primary cultural dimensions (e.g., power to distance, uncertainty avoidance, individual versus collectivism, and male versus female) (Ailon, 2008; Pearlson & Saunders, 2010). The dimensions can project a Western value orientation, but the addition of short-term versus long-term, performance, and humane orientations would provide a more global perspective on an organization's culture.

This book elucidated the cultural value dimensions relative to a diverse knowledge worker population in a large county governmental agency, which are pervasive in similarly situated governmental organizations. The research design in the qualitative case study on change management included empirical materials collection, sampling, and analysis methods. Each step in the process was important in the construction of a foundation for subsequent steps.

The use of the methods of empirical materials collection supported the analysis and presentation of material conclusions in Chapter 4 and outlined the relationship of the outcomes to the methods. By culling each knowledge worker's experience in isolation from other workers, a greater comprehension of the whole was apparent.

Chapter 4

Analysis and Results

This book's purpose sought to explore organizational and leadership components that contribute to the creation of an innovative culture and the experiences of 21 purposively selected management knowledge workers in a county in the State of Minnesota. The deployment of a qualitative method and single case study research design led to the isolation and identification of organizational patterns of behavior and related themes aligned with study participant experiences. This research approach also yielded a potential benefit in the recognition of various governmental knowledge worker value dimensions inherent to all governmental agencies' culture and climate. The data collection produced potential benefits relative to the recognition of the county's organizational change readiness and capability maturity relating to the development of innovative service offerings and solutions to address the need of county residents. A description of the chosen research design and methods was presented in Chapter 3.

Descriptions of the study findings articulated in Chapter 4 include sample, demographic information, data collection processes, data analysis, presentation of findings, and results summary. The primary research assumption was that leadership affects the organizational culture and climate, which in turn serves as the most reliable predictor in the production of innovative solutions to address the needs of county residents. The chapter concludes with a summary of book results from the perspective of the research questions.

Operational Problems examined

The general problem in many governmental agencies' is structuring innovative service delivery models for social and entitlement programs to meet the needs of citizens within the programmatic reality of shrinking agency budgets (Walker, 2005). Structural considerations relate to the programmatic service and leadership functions that reside in the purview of an agency. The operational design aspects relates to the execution of those functions and determining the appropriate mix of internal and external resources to perform service delivery tasks (Robichau, 2011).

The specific problem is that the organizational culture in government agencies can present operational and leadership barriers to knowledge workers in determining cost-efficient, effective, and innovative service programs that respond appropriately and adapt to a mandated set of constituent social needs. Ancillary issues relating to the structural problem also extend to determining the appropriate mix of services offerings relative to constituents' changing life situations. These stimuli arise from a series of complex social variables that include the constituents receiving services and the government workforce possessing the task of executing programmatic policies and procedures in an ever-changing landscape.

Purpose of this book

The purpose of this book's qualitative research was to examine the operational (e.g., leadership) interactions and cultural barriers of various programmatic actors (e.g., knowledge workers, residents, community partners, and community stakeholders) engaged in the delivery of program services and to explore how those interactive relationships precipitate in the deployment of service delivery mechanisms for governmental programs. The results from this book may indicate the complex adaptive system behavior of governmental agencies and provide an understanding of each actor's perspectives using a complexity theory model. This model assessed the nonlinear effect that environmental changes have on each actor's operation and how those nonlinear effects forms the basis for subsystem self-organization to achieve desired outcomes.

The descriptive single case study research design involved studying operational models of organizational change as well as leadership behavior variables found in the largest local government agency in the state of Minnesota where change events are prevalent. The descriptive theory the design encompasses is leadership behaviors relative to change events are the greater predictors of success and creating a culture of collaboration, cooperation, knowledge sharing, and innovation.

Study Context

This was a case study research project to determine what leadership characteristics allow successful completion of creative change initiatives and promotes an organizational culture that embraces innovation through collaboration, cooperation, and knowledge sharing within knowledge worker communities of practice. Previous research on leadership behavior patterns advances a theory that the development of innovative work cultures is dependent on organizational leaders' understanding of the value dimensions of the prevailing culture (de Mooij & Hofstede, 2011). These cultural value dimensions are power to distance, uncertainty avoidance, individualism versus collectivism, male versus female, and short-term versus long-term orientation (Hofstede & Minkov, 2010). The literature on organizational work system performance suggests these value dimensions can have an impact on team and individual worker's engagement in the achievement of enterprise goals and objectives relative to change.

In a constantly changing world, having an understanding of these cultural dimensions provides leaders at every level (e.g., upper, middle, and line managers) with a more global perspective of an organizational ecosystem. This study explored the effect of these dimensions relative to a diverse knowledge worker population at the county, which may be pervasive in other governmental organizations (de Mooij & Hofstede, 2011; Hofstede & Minkov, 2010).

This study also examined functionalist and anthropological leadership perspectives. The functionalist perspective posits a notion that leaders architect culture change by way of substantive or visible action or the symbolic organizational roles a leader executes. Conversely, an anthropological viewpoint advances a passive participant role and questions a leader's ability to affect the culture (i.e., leaders are part of culture, not apart from it) (Karp & Helgø, 2008; Kotter, 1998).

Research Questions

There were four open-ended questions designed to simulate thoughts and subjective responses in three focus groups and nine individual interview sessions. Responses to these questions advanced a board range of opinions for analysis to determine common value themes and operational structure preferences.

The four general topic areas that the case study focus group and individual interview participants addressed were as follows:

Define the organizational culture here at the county and what are the key components and change opportunities?

What are key leadership components you feel are necessary to promote innovation change, workflow collaboration, and knowledge sharing?

Responsive government: What does the term mean relative to operational or intuitional change and how would you know that you have mobilized organizational resources to achieve it?

What is the appropriate role for external partners and communities of interest in the operation of governmental agency workflows and how they should be structured?

Each focus group and individual interview session was presented four questions that were designed to elucidate study participant's subjective response to the general topic area. The questions and related follow-up was also designed to explore their personal interactions with the leadership phenomenon and its effect on organizational culture.

Participant Samples

Demographic profiles of the participants representing the study sample were arranged by gender, generational classification, academic preparation, and degree focus. Accessibility and selection of research study participants was contingent on adherence to specific criteria that included management and supervisory level knowledge workers. Preference factors for participant selection included criteria such as the number of years of employment and organizational management level. The final sample of 21 participants received advance copies of the four questions prior to the focus group and interview meetings to allow sufficient time to understand the questions and collect their thoughts about their lived experiences.

Prior to each focus group or interview session, the researcher provided an overview of the study purpose, collection of the signed informed consent, and verification that study participation included agreement to the audiotaping of the sessions. Attentiveness and awareness of the details of participants' verbal and nonverbal responses for each question was a key component to minimize the need for validation during data analysis. Follow-up questions were asked if needed to assist in clarifying responses to any specific question before proceeding to the next question.

Sampling approach

The study involved deployment of a nonprobability type of sampling that resulted in a convenience sample of the county management team (Rubin, 2008; Willis, 2007). The purposive sample of participants included four participants in each of the three county management focus groupings (i.e., upper, middle, and line supervisors) and nine individual staff interviews. Obtaining a smaller number of focus group participants might provide sufficient opportunity for staff to be heard and to express their opinions in a nonthreatening setting (Yin, 2009).

Characteristics of the focus group participants included a representation from two generation (i.e., Baby-boomer and Gen X), and gender diversity. The current case study research project included a selection of knowledge workers from the executive branch of the county and included appointed and elected officials, (i.e., commissioners and administrators). Middle management knowledge workers consisted of program directors, area managers, and program area managers.

Line staff supervisors completed the sample and consisted of functional process managers and subject matter experts. The purposeful sampling selection criteria for participants included generation, tenure, educational and technical background, employment diversity, and supervisory background components. The intent of this sampling method was to ensure the selection of a sufficient cross-section of knowledge workers to provide a base of experience and operational viewpoints.

Employees chosen for staff interviews displayed similar sample characteristics but additionally had a county employment history exceeding 10 years. Employees with 10 or more years of tenure have more familiarity with the county's operational culture and climate because of their interactions with three or more county administrative leaders. This tenure also demonstrates significant change acceptance tendencies.

Demographic profiles of participants

The following paragraphs reflect biographical overviews of each of the 21 participants purposively selected for the research study. Participants were expected to represent the contextual perspective relative to their direct and indirect experiences involving change at the county and its desire to foster an innovative workplace environment. Each subject was assigned management level group identification (e.g., MG1-3) and a participant number based on focus group or individual interview participation (e.g., FG 1-4 or IV1-3). The numbering schema corresponded to the ordered sequence of their study participation invitation acceptance. This nomenclature was used to identify the subject in each profile and elsewhere in this study.

Participant profiles

MG1-FG1: He is a county administrator. He holds a Juris Doctorate (JD) and has been responsible for several change initiatives relating to improving operational efficiency. His areas of responsibility included the information and communication technology function. He is regarded by many staff as a transformational leader, although he does not self-describe as such. He considers the county to be in a transitional state given the organizational ecosystem and the required county response.

MG1-FG2: Her title is Human Services Area Director, and she also holds a JD and her area of responsibility includes direct services to clients in the form of assistance and medical care. She has held this position for 10 years. She had recently taken on a project to facilitate a change in the department's service delivery model and regionalization of service offerings.

MG1-FG3: Her title is Chief Information Officer, and she has a Master's degree in computer science. Her area of responsibilities includes the centralized information and communication technologies functions. Current change initiatives include completing the county's move to a federated enterprise model from the previous decentralized model for the county's 26 business lines.

MG1-FG4: His title is Assistant Administrator and director of the county's Human Services (HS) department. He has a Master's degree in social sciences and his areas of responsibility include human service and public health. The most recent change initiatives include the operationalizing of the client services delivery model and site development. He is also a results only workplace environment (ROWE) champion.

MG1-IV1: His title is Chief Financial Officer and director of the Office of Budget & Finance. He has a Master's degree in management and finance and has a certified public accountant designation. His recent change initiatives include the procurement and implementation of an enterprise resource planning (ERP) application. He has also led the county's business intelligence application planning and implementation.

MG1-IV2: Her title is Director of Internal Audit, and she holds a Bachelor's degree in business and Certified Internal Auditor and Certified Public Accountant designations. In addition to compliance auditing for county programs, her area is responsibility for process improvement relating to transaction execution. Recent change initiatives include ERP procurement and the installation of compliance tracking software to assist in the completion of special audits.

MG1-IV3: His title is county commissioner, which is an elected position. He has a JD, and he has had Board Technology Committee chair responsibilities. He has also occupied the county board chairmanship for four terms and represents two of the more affluent suburbs in the county. His past work experience includes some of the state's largest and most recognized enterprises (e.g., 3M and Dayton Hudson). His most recent change pet projects include introduction to the balanced scorecard approach to county operations.

MG2-FG1: He is an information technology manager, and he holds a Bachelor's degree in business. He has responsibility for the imaging functions in HS which provides the content for the department's electronic case file (ECF) application and the county-wide accounts payable invoice imaging system. His area also provides operational support for the deployment of the ECF application to non-program areas (e.g., finance).

MG2-FG2: She is a senior manager in the county's Public Works business line and she holds a Master's degree in business. Her area of responsibility includes the general administration of the business that covers procurement, capital budgeting, and workforce planning. Her most recent change initiative is the county-wide restructure of the procurement function to streamline the process to improve efficiency and effectiveness.

MG2-FG3: He is a Human Services Area Manager and he holds a Master's degree in social science. His area of responsibilities includes initial point of entry for clients seeking financial assistance and housing related services. His recent change initiative includes the development of a boarder needs assessment application that serves as a comprehensive data gathering tool to allow workers to pinpoint multiple client needs at the first encounter.

MG2-FG4: He is a senior manager in the Taxpayer Services business line and he holds a Bachelor's degree in computer science. His area of responsibility includes property tax collections for the county and the related systems. His most recent change effort was the implementation of a new system to facilitate the collection, recording, and reporting of tax collections. This system also provides a web service interface that publishes information about the county's taxable properties to real estate search engines and regulatory entities.

MG2-IV1: He is a Human Services Area Manager and he holds a Bachelor's in Public Administration. His area of responsibilities includes child support enforcement and collection.

In addition to administering federal and state assistance programs to help persons in need of financial or health care assistance, food support, or emergency assistance.

MG2-IV2: She is a Human Services program manager, and she holds a Bachelor's degree in Social Work. Her area of focus is in protective services for children and adults. Her change focus to date includes expansion of the BNA tool and adoption to regionalization.

MG2-IV3: She is a Quality Manager in the county's health plan business line, and she holds a Bachelor's degree in liberal arts. Her area is devoted to programmatic improvement in the county's health plan offering. In particular as they relate to adherence to care protocols. Her current change initiative relates to the Affordable Healthcare Act implementation.

MG3-FG1: He is a Program Manager/E in the Human Services Financial Analysis and Accounting area. He holds a Bachelor's degree in business and his area of responsibility includes provider contract administration and compliance. He recently led an implementation of a system to track provider contract compliance. He is also a ROWE champion.

MG3-FG2: She is a unit supervisor in the county corrections area and she holds a Bachelor's in Social Sciences. Her area of responsibly is collaborating with criminal justice partners, community-based organizations, and volunteers and interns to supervise and deliver sustainable correctional services to adult and juvenile offenders. Recent change initiatives include a review of recidivism rates and the impact of community based interventions.

MG3-FG3: She is a Human Services supervisor in the Work Supports area, and she holds a Bachelor's degree in Psychology. Her area administers childcare assistance, job search and job counseling and training programs that assist in supporting employment and self-sufficiency for unemployed or underemployed persons. Recent change initiative relate to ROWE and its workflow effect.

MG3-FG4: He is a Corrections unit supervisor and, he holds a Master's in public administration. His area of responsibility in the Department of Community Corrections and Rehabilitation includes collaboration with external agencies to provide services for adult and juvenile offenders from the jail to the community. Most recent change initiative involves a move to community-based supports.

MG3-IV1: She is a Program Analysis supervisor in the Supportive Housing area, and she holds a Ph.D. in Social Sciences. Her area of responsibilities includes housing for the homeless. This includes strategies to address episodic and temporal gaps in client supportive housing as well as services for project and community-based, affordable housing initiatives. Recent change initiatives include the implementation of ROWE and CSDM.

MG3-IV2: He is a Correction unit supervisor, and he holds a Bachelor's in Social Science. He has responsibilities in the area of juvenile crisis intervention. This unit provides child protection workers who determine if enforcement reports fit within the statutory definitions of child abuse and neglect. If a child is determined not to be safe at their parental home, placement of the child outside the home is considered. Recent changes in the community-based approach are the primary focus of this unit.

MG3-IV3: He is a manager in the human resources department, and he holds a Master's degree in business. His area of responsibility includes employee compensation and job classification reviews. Recent change efforts include ROWE and its effect of contract negotiations with the county's labor unions.

The following graphs illustrate participant dispersion along gender, generation, degree level, and degree emphasis.

Population sample dispersion characteristics

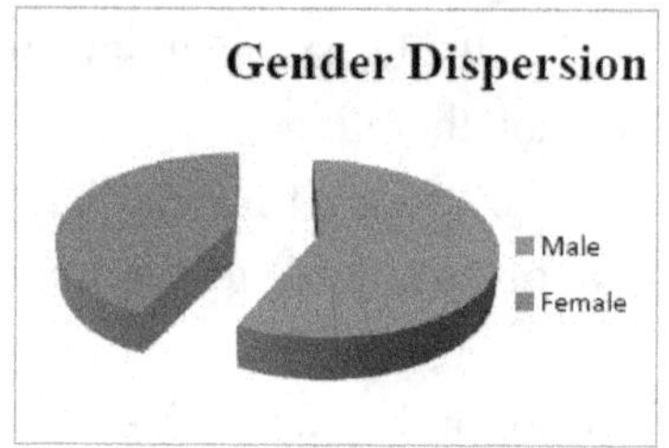

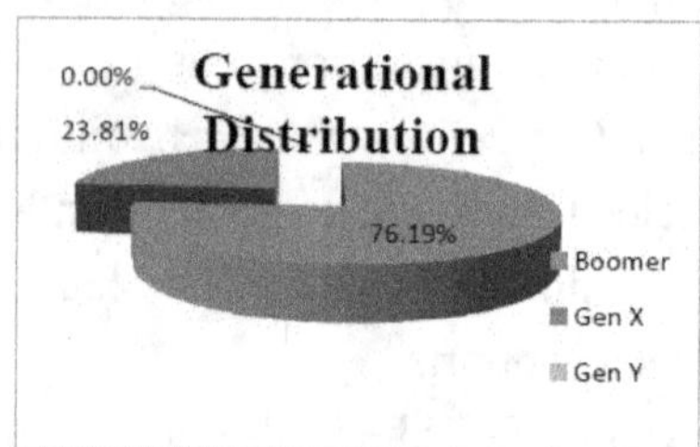

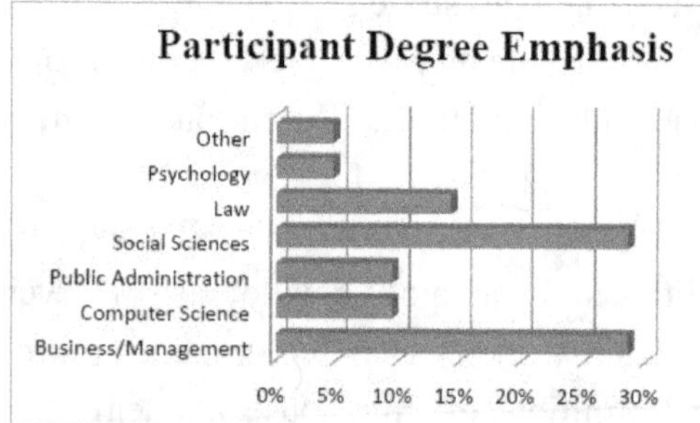

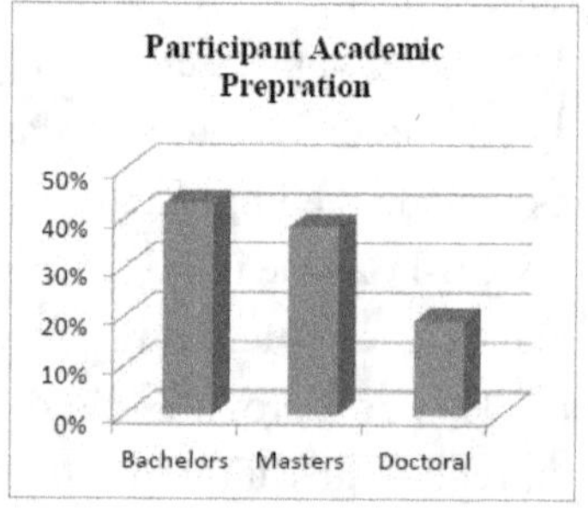

Data Collection procedures

Several data types (i.e., field notes, transcriptions, and digital recordings) were collected to ensure triangulation of study results. Each focus group and individual interview session audiotape files were labeled with a code to correlate with each management focus group and each participant was assigned a code in place of proper names to ensure anonymity and confidentiality. All taped group and interview sessions were transcribed into a Microsoft Word document format. The data collection phase consisted of conducting three focus group meeting with four participants in each group, and individual interviews with three participants from each management grouping (i.e., upper, middle, and line).

The recording device was placed on in a central location (e.g., conference table) to ensure vocal accuracy and correctness of transcriptions. The data collection phase included transmission of the recorded sessions to a third party transcription service for conversion into Microsoft Word documents for analysis. The data gathered from participant responses was sufficient to frame and articulate the lived experience of the knowledge workers, such that the researcher was no longer acquiring or exposed to new information (Schwandt, 2007). The study incorporated an adoption of the modified van Kaam method for phenomenological data analysis by Moustakas (1994).

The data collection process involved taped and transcribed interviews that captured participant impressions in the course of the focus group and individual interview queries. The application of the modified van Kaam method (Moustakas, 1994) and use of the NVivo 10 software (QSR International, 2012) facilitated data analysis and identification of emerging themes and patterns from the interactions of the 21 county management knowledge workers. The deployment of qualitative software, such as NVivo 10 increases the validity of the research study for the reason that the software features provides for the easy uploading, handling, coding, grouping, and sorting of voice-recorded data and Microsoft word documents (Schönfelder, 2011).

The focus group meetings and individual interviews were tape recorded using an Olympus Digital Voice Recorder VN-702PC device. The audio recorded sessions were transcribed into Microsoft Word formatted document using an external transcription service and imported into the NVivo 10 computer software. NVivo 10 software features provided for management of data, such as visual reading of transcripts and coding of the data (Schönfelder, 2011).

The collected focus group and interview data was analyzed using phenomenological methods designed by van Kaam and modified by Moustakas (1994). Deployment of the phenomenological method of analysis involved a sequential steps procedure that provided the foundation for an inclusive individual and group description of the essence of the leadership phenomenon. A pilot group of three county knowledge workers was used to review the research questions prior to inclusion in the initial e-mail solicitation. The focus group and individual interview sessions were 60 minutes in length. Participant familiarity with the research questions allowed better preparation for sessions and produced timely and substantial discourse on the internationality of important aspects of the County's operational culture.

Each of the focus group and individual interview participant sessions were completed and recorded from the beginning to the last research question absent any interruptions during the data gathering group and interview process. Participants were provided the opportunity to express freely any perceptions regarding the composition and construct of the research questions. The data collection transcription and coding process was as follows:

Transcription and Coding

The deployment of NVivo 10 qualitative software facilitated the categorization and compilation of word frequency counts and statistical information aggregation after the data was encoded. The NVivo 10 features provided assistance in the analysis of the collected data and provided the mechanism for managing, organizing, and coding data, but did not analyze study findings (Baxter & Jack, 2008; DiCicco-Bloom & Crabtree, 2006). An example in the use of NVivo10 features would be during the seven-step analysis process of the Van Kaam's modified method, NVivo software features facilitated to the Horizonalization process by allowing the visualization, handling and reallocation of selected participant's interview statements (Chorba, 2011; Robinson, 2014).

The NVivo 10 software facilitated the Reduction process by allowing easy removal of information from study participant statements. The data transcription process consisted of the transcription of participants recorded interviews. The initial process involved transmission of the audio files to an external transcription service for translation into Microsoft Word formatted documents. Transcribing tape-recorded meetings into text can be problematic in terms of the accuracy of third-party transcribed data.

Third-party transcribers can have functional difficulties during the capture of spoken words in a text format because of sentence context or structure, quotation use, word omissions and mistaking words or phrases for similar words. People can often converse in run-on sentences, which places transcribers in the position of making judgment calls on spoken words. Quotation mark insertion (e.g., periods or commas) can also alter the meaning intent of entire sentences (Petty, Thomson, & Stew, 2012; Schönfelder, 2011; Yin, 2009).

According to Yin, (2009), when a researcher is working with audio data transcriptions, it is advisable to review the audiotape several times while comparing the written transcriptions to ensure accuracy during interpretation. This method was employed by the researcher during this book's execution. Subsequent steps included listening to the recorded focus group and individual interview sessions from the Olympus Digital Voice Recorder device, and manually correcting any transcription errors or word use from each recorded to the transcription service provided in the Microsoft Word document format.

Data elements such as names of participants or ancillary organizations were removed during the transcription reconciliation process. The NVivo 10 software program provided for the uploading of word documents as well as voice recording files. The data coding process was initiated when the recorded focus group and individual interviews and transcribed MS word documents from study participants were uploaded in the NVivo 10 program. NVivo 10 encoding features provided for the color coding of the MS word transcripts. Once the data coding was completed, a modified van Kaam method was used for further analysis.

Data Analysis and Presentation of Findings

The modified van Kaam method provided assistance with the data analysis of the study with a qualitative method and phenomenological single case study research design. Deployment of the modified van Kaam method involves a phenomenology process of analyzing the interviews, which provided insight and the achievement of deeper understanding of the meaning and essence of the phenomenon or experience under study (Mahoney, 2010; Römer, 2012; Symington, 2012). The identification and development of meaning through emerging patterns and meaning units (i.e., themes) related to the innovative solution creation phenomena from the lived experiences of 21 management knowledge workers involved in change processes.

This book focused on exploration of innovative solution creation and the effect of leadership by conducting group and interview sessions. The purpose of the sessions was to gain insight about the perceived behavioral elements that might enable or inhibit the creation of innovative service delivery systems using the van Kaam method modified by Moustakas (1994). Use of the van Kaam method requires the construction of categories and perceived key elements such as leadership, organizational culture, and external environment required organization to facilitate the flow of information, identification of meaning regarding the phenomenon, analysis of the data, and identification of themes.

The Moustakas modification of van Kaam's method for data analysis involves seven steps: horizonalization, reduction, clustering and thematizing, validation, individual textural description, individual structural description, and combined textural-structural description (Robinson, 2014; Römer, 2012). The following paragraphs contain a description of this seven step data analysis process and its application to this book. Qualitative data analysis is inductive and may involve going from specific-transcripts and field-notes to identification of emergent themes. Such themes may emerge from the evaluation of statements fitting significant categories of related data elements (Baxter & Jack, 2008; Newman, 2005; Schwandt, 2007).

Step 1: Horizonalization

The first step of Moustakas' modification of van Kaam's seven-step data analysis process involves the manual analysis of the data. Horizonalization is an important component in the phenomenological reduction process and involves the placement of equal value on all individual lived experiences of the participants regarding the phenomenon. The Horizonalization analysis process involves the collection of words, sentences, or examples of expressions contained in encoded transcripts. The criteria used to determine the significance of a word, sentence or phase was based on the identification of participant responses that corresponds to a desired event.

The process of listening to the session recordings several times assisted the researcher in the comparison and consistency between the recordings of each focus group and individual interview information collected. The textual words and sentences within each transcript were categorized and noted for further identification of themes (Schwandt, 2007). Some words or statements collected from participant responses and related to the study research such as "command and control", "compliance culture", "widget focused management", "risk aversion", and "constituent facing" were noted with a purpose of identifying patterns and common use of these terms among the study participants. Several of these comments illustrated cultural value dimensions (e.g., uncertainty avoidance or collective versus individual).

Step 2: Reduction

The data reduction step focuses on the reduction and elimination of irrelevant, redundant, or vague statements. The key determinate during the reduction step was to ensure that data from participant responses was correctly allocated into invariant constituent categories. Using NVivo 10 software features, selected data from transcribed transcripts was allocated in child nodes. The use of child nodes facilitated the reading and review of data contained on the nodes. The reduction process was done by asking questions about the data contained on the nodes.

If the data described participant's lived experiences or opinions that explained components of the innovation and leadership phenomenon, and the data fit into a category list, a theme was considered to have been identified (Mahoney, 2010; Römer, 2012). If the data did not explain the experience and did not accommodate itself to a category list, the data was not included as part of a theme. An example of this allocation happened when a participant stated "staff engagement is critical. I also think the vision is critical" resulted in the statement assignment to the invariant constituent labeled "change management" under a theme labeled "leadership."

Step 3: Clustering and Thematizing

The third step involved the clustering and thematizing of invariant constituents. The remaining statements from the reduction process were clustered into labeled thematic groupings (Robinson, 2014; Römer, 2012; Stake, 2010). Review of encoded transcripts as well as the further elimination of data not related to the purpose of the research study provided for the identification of categories and core themes (Stake, 2010; Symington, 2012). Using NVivo 10 software features, the combination of coding using words, phrases, text-string searches, and the exploration of textual patterns (e.g., word trees) facilitated the linking and labeling of themes. An example of this word tree analysis is presented in the figure below.

Nvivo Word Tree

The data was organized based on the 21 participants from the three focus group meetings and nine individual interview transcripts. The manual review and comparison of words or sentences from participant response to a research question helped in the identification and elaboration of short phrases. An example on the organization of data was in the use of annotated words or short phrases such as "organic change", "leadership relationships.", "culture of compliance", "risk aversion", and "innovative work environment" that were identified and noted in the session transcripts. Labeling the short phrases facilitated the grouping of information based on participants responses related to the research phenomenon. The grouped data was scanned for categories of the research phenomenon and possible relationships among the categories. Similar units of meaning were also grouped into categories (Bhattacherjee, 2012; Chorba, 2011; Schwandt, 2007; Stake, 2010).

Some questions such as "what leadership components promotes innovative change", "define the key components of the county's culture", "define responsive government", and "what role does external stimuli play in the county processes" assisted the emergence and distribution of categories. The categories that resulted were labeled. The selection of a core category was based on the consistency of the participant statements and similar meanings. Core categories emerged from the collection of participants who stated that the leadership relationship is important to a knowledge worker's behavior or that less innovative work environments might develop because of an unsupportive or risk-averse leadership structure.

The allocation of themes as nodes assisted in the mapping of information, which facilitated the interpretation and meaning of the data. The textual descriptions of individual participants were evaluated to make certain that each interview response was properly allocated to the invariant constituent (Petty, Thomson, & Stew, 2012). An example might be, if a study participant stated, "within the confines of what county government is, it would be hard to argue that The county can be transformational", this participant's response would be allocated to an invariant constituent "external constraint" and themed under "responsive government." A similar process was also applied to participants whom, as an example had "risk aversion to worker empowerment" as a barrier to transactional trust. The themes constitute the core elements of the experience of the participant. Grouping the clusters provided development of textual descriptions and emergence of core themes. The emergent themes were innovative workplace, leadership, organizational culture, and external stimuli.

A data model representing the free node allocation process is presented in the figure below.

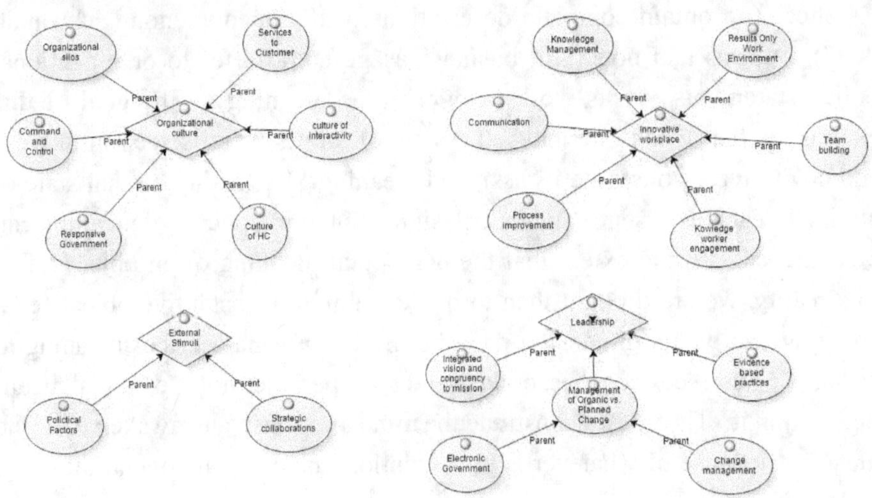

Free node allocation

The allocation of responses to invariant constituent nodes is consistent with qualitative analysis of intentionality, noema, and noesis. This allocation is also consistent with the complex adaptive system perspective of this book. This concept of transcendental phenomenology acknowledges the complexity in gaining an understanding of human science and in searches for knowledge in research investigations. In addition to the resurrection of philosophical debates between analytic versus transcendental practitioners, as it relates to the question of language preceding meaning as opposed to meaning preceding language (Moustakas, 1994; Petty, Thomson, & Stew, 2012; Schwandt, 2007). The crux of this debate is whether meaning is embedded in the experience itself or is an outgrowth of reflection and afterthought. Intentionality directs or orients consciousness toward something (real or imaginary, actual or nonexistent). General agreement exists that meaning is at the core of perception, remembrance, judgment, feeling, and thought (Petty, Thomson, & Stew, 2012; Schwandt, 2007; Stake, 2010).

Noema is that which is experienced in the textual or descriptive sense, noesis is the structural or cognitive manner in which it is experienced. Both terms refer to meanings and are a way of emphasizing and reinforcing acquisition of knowledge found in those meanings, rather than in the analysis of the physical objects (Römer, 2012; Stake, 2010; Schwandt, 2007). The reflection on what one has "seen", will allow one to grasp concealed meanings in a state of affairs. The challenge is to systemically revisit that state of affairs to reflect and obtain complete descriptions of the phenomenon (Schwandt, 2007). Noesis and noema in business usage could refer to organizational policy statements versus work practices type meanings. The goal of this exercise is that when one looks at a state of affairs what is seen intuitively and cogitatively constitute its assigned meaning. Reflecting on that state of affairs to reach its essence and unlock significant components of meaning can be achieved. To the extent that the perceptual meaning of an object refers to a reality, we are thought then to be describing a substantive object (e.g., adhering to a value dimension or policy). The noema ascribes meaning to "what" a person sees, touches, or feels and all experience holds essential meanings within it. The noeses constitute the mind and spirit, and awaken us to the meaning or sense of whatever is in perception, memory, judgment, thinking, and feeling.

Noesis refers to the way in which the "what" is experienced, the experience or act of experiencing, the subject-correlate. It adheres to the act of perception, sensation, thought, recollection, or judgment; all of which are rooted with meanings. The noeses bring into experience the consciousness of something. In and through the noeses objects appear, shine forward, and arc "rationally" determined. The noema corresponds at all points to the noesis, such that one cannot exist without the other. The noema, in perception, is its perceptual meaning or the perceived as such; in recollection, the remembered as such; in judging, the judged as such (e.g., empirical value). Noema is that which is experienced, "the what" of experience, the object-correlate. To the extent that the perceptual meaning of an object refers to a reality (desired or negotiated), we are describing a real thing. The description of a thing incorporates its meaning (Nenon, 2012; Robinson, 2014; Symington, 2012).

Step 4: Validation

The fourth step provided the means for confirmation and validation of the themes with the transcription of each participant. Each transcribed and encoded group meeting and individual interview session represented the essence of the participant's perception and lived experience related to the phenomena of organizational innovation and leadership. The themes were validated by review of the entire transcript of each participant or group to determine if those themes were clearly expressed or easily comparable. Themes identified as unclear or easily incompatible were considered irrelevant and removed. Core themes that represented Innovative Workplace, Leadership, External Stimuli, and Organizational Culture were validated by interpreting the data from the meetings and interviews. The responses supported the validity of the invariant constituent and theme.

Step 5: Individual Textural Description

The fifth step focused on developing individual textural description of the experience (Nenon, 2012). Textural description process was done by extracting verbatim examples of how participants described the essential qualities and characteristics of the leadership experience and its effect on fostering a culture that embraces change and the production of innovative solutions to service delivery. The interpretation of the textural analysis of the transcribed interviews resulted from the findings extracted from the textual data of the participant's verbatim responses. Each individual textural analysis was represented by accurate examples of participant's experiences and perceptions about leadership's effect on the development of an innovative work environment. The significant statements or thematic data provides the description of what (noema) the study participants experienced.

Step 6: Individual Structural Description

The sixth step involved the individual structural descriptions of the experiences of the 21 study participants. The development of the structural descriptions required using a process that required the application of imagination to the way of thinking and attitudes of knowledge worker professionals. The development of the structural description for each study participant was based on the combination of participant interview experiences and field notes collected during the individual interviews. The use of the field notes provided to account for the feelings, beliefs, and perceived behavior of participants during the interview.

The individual structural description provides an account of the underlying dynamics of the experience, the themes and qualities account for the context or setting (noesis) connected with the phenomenon and what conditions evoked the experience (Chorba, 2011; Creswell, 2007; Moustakas, 1994; Nenon, 2012; Stake, 2010). The individual structural descriptions are important to the purpose of the study because of the underlying feelings, reflections, and emotions associated with the perceptions of the participant and the lived experiences of the leadership effect on innovation. The individual structural descriptions were built using imaginative variation identified in the transcript-verbatim and field notes impressions that permeated the participants' experiences to reflect the essence of the phenomenon (Stake, 2010).

Step 7: Combined Textural-Structural Description

The final step in the van Kaam method of analysis consisted of elaborating a textural-structural narrative of the meanings and essence of views, opinions, perception, and experiences from each study participant. The core themes that emerged from the combination of views, opinions, and experiences represented the whole group (Robinson, 2014; Stake, 2010). This combined description represents the common experience of all study participants and is defined as the essential quality, invariant structure, or substance of the observed phenomenon (Baxter & Jack, 2008; Creswell, 2007). This final step requires the researcher to deploy interpretive anthropological methods to develop the cultural orientation of the organization (Baxter & Jack, 2008; Schwandt, 2007). This cultural orientation was defined by organizational patterns of behavior forming its ideational system, which encompasses the shared knowledge and understanding of group members (Schwandt, 2007).

Emergent Themes

The process involved in the relational analysis of collected data began with the concept identification as presented in a given text or series of texts. Such texts were composed of words or sentences contained on the transcript data. The identification of concepts was followed by the observation of any re-occurrences related to explicit concepts using a clustering technique. Meaningful concepts were grouped to determine spatial relationships. Grouping interrelated concepts resulted in the emergence of themes. The data analysis provided a means of exploring the invariant constituents for the thematic categories, which provided statistical data from the lived experience of 21 knowledge workers. Invariant constituents are the horizons that remain from the experience, and thematic categories that might be defined as non-repetitive, non-overlapping, labeled constituents clustered into themes of the experience (Römer, 2012; Yin, 2009).

Four themes evolved from the data analysis of the research study. The emergent themes were:

Innovative Workplace

Leadership

External stimuli
Organizational Culture

Combined Textural-Structural Description

A composite description of the leadership effect on organizational culture defines a universal or unified statement of the phenomenon typified by the interrelated, coherent experiences of all the participants (Römer, 2012; Symington, 2012). The composite description provided the essences of the phenomenon, and because all individuals experienced the phenomenon, the essentials of the experiences are invariant (Nenon, 2012; Stake, 2010; Symington, 2012). For this book, the phenomenon (noema) was the fostering of an enterprise-wide innovative workplace in which knowledge workers were engaged in delivery of creative solutions to county residents. The perceptions held by knowledge workers relative to components of that innovative workplace (noesis) were also articulated during this book execution. The synthesized textural and structural descriptions contain the deeper meanings inherent in the experiences of the participants collectively.

Data Explication

The results of the reflexive, in-depth data analysis describe how the participants experienced change relative to leadership involvement. The outcomes from the analysis of individual research questions served as patterns when subsequently analyzing all questions. The clustering from the subsequent analysis revealed four core themes, numerous patterns, and outliers consisting of secondary meaning units.

The combined textual description of the leadership phenomenon and its effect on the development of an innovative culture can be demonstrated by the experiences of the 21 study participants as they have been embroiled in several change initiatives. Case studies must show sufficient evidence to convince the reader that the case has been explored in-depth (Baxter & Jack, 2008; Neuman, 2005; Yin, 2009). One way in which this can be accomplished is through the use of multiple sources of evidence (Schwandt, 2007; Yin, 2009).

In the context of this book, the composite description from the research participants indicates that the county does not have a dominant culture that guides its workforce to a common set of goals and objectives relative to developing innovative service delivery options. The participants readily acknowledged that the leadership in various program areas can varies based on the operational configuration of a particular area and the personal behaviors of the area leadership. The transactional requirements of governmental operations create a compliance driven culture necessitated by the expectations of external stimuli (e.g., federal and state governments, constituents, and community partners). This transactional mindset is evident in administrative support areas or functions that are responsible for disbursing and controlling revenue streams (e.g., finance or human resources). An essential component of this compliance culture is the notion of value-added service and giving constituents a greater return for the tax dollars the county receives.

Those program areas dealing with the human services functions tend to display some elements of transformational behavior in that responses to client needs do not always follow prescribed programmatic structures. In those cases there can be some latitude in the delivery mechanism for services, which allows for creativity in terms of partnerships, alternative delivery vehicles, and use of revenue streams. Robust constituent involvement is also prevalent in the human services area, which translates into responsiveness from area leadership.

The county understands the value of creating an environment that promotes collaboration, cooperation, and knowledge sharing as a mechanism for addressing the needs of constituents, delivering value-added services, and maintaining its fiduciary responsibilities. The county has instituted several initiatives to improve its workplace climate (e.g., ROWE) and renewed its Diversity and Inclusion Program to emphasize the value the county's places on diverse opinions in the problem solving process.

The structural context of the County's leadership in development of an innovative culture remains somewhat fragmented because some areas of the County has leaders who are risk averse and exhibit high degrees of command and control orientation. This type of orientation inhibits worker empowerment and task ownership, which in turn affects performance and building transactional trust between workers and leaders (Brake, 2008; Jamrog Vickers, & Bear, 2006). Several participants remarked on this point as being generational in its presentation and that the creation of a shared culture that embraces change and innovation will not occur in the current management configuration. This finding is consistent with the literature in that the next generation of worker will demand greater workplace cohesion, meaningful tasks, and more of a voice in how work is structured and performed (Page & Vella-Brodrick, 2009; Pratt, 2010; Robert, Dennis, Alan, & Hung, 2009).

Summary

The purpose of this book and its qualitative method and phenomenological research design was to explore the leadership phenomenon and its effect on producing an innovative organizational culture that responds creatively to the programmatic needs of citizens. The study participants are 21 management professional knowledge workers currently employed by a local government agency. An aim of the research was to identify emergent themes that might help identify the conditions that contribute to an organizational culture that embraces change and develops innovative solutions to operational problems or opportunities. The study involved the use of open-ended interview questions, audio-taping, and transcription of the interview and focus group sessions.

The seven-step approach as articulated by Moustakas (1994) was deployed to analyze the data. The analysis of transcribed interviews and focus groups was done by using the modified van Kaam method according to Moustakas (1994) and NVivo 10 qualitative software. The NVivo 10 software was used to explore the textual descriptions from the study participant sessions. The featured query methods assisted in accurate identification of themes. The four emergent themes were innovative workplace, leadership, external stimuli, and organizational culture. Chapter 5 will include answers to the research question, implications of the findings, significance to leadership, conclusions, and recommendations.

Chapter 5

Conclusions and Recommendations

The purpose of the current qualitative phenomenological research project was to examine theories of leadership and organizational culture factors perceived by knowledge workers facing potential issues and difficulties in developing innovative solutions to change related programmatic initiatives. The current research study was designed to study the reactions and explore factors that may affect the reception and acceptance of organizational knowledge workers to new enterprise changes and process transformation. The depth of this study is inherent in the knowledge gathered from individuals who experienced change events in the largest county government agency in Minnesota.

The current research project facilitated the discovery of anecdotal observations, emotions, and feelings from supervisory knowledge workers manifested by change events in the county operational structure and its prevailing culture. Chapter 5 includes an interpretation of the data analysis results reported in Chapter 4 and is organized as follows: implications and outcomes of research questions, analysis of study results, implications and significance of the finding, recommendations for future research, and conclusion.

Chapter 5 also includes outcomes of the research questions. The four research questions were designed to expose the real-life experience, perceptions, and feelings of the focus group and individual interview study participants. Chapter 5 also includes recommendations for future research, leadership initiatives in governmental agencies, and a summary of the current research. As part of the recommendation to leadership in governmental agencies seeking to create innovative work environments, the following model was created to illustrate the interplay of major components in a government ecosystem.

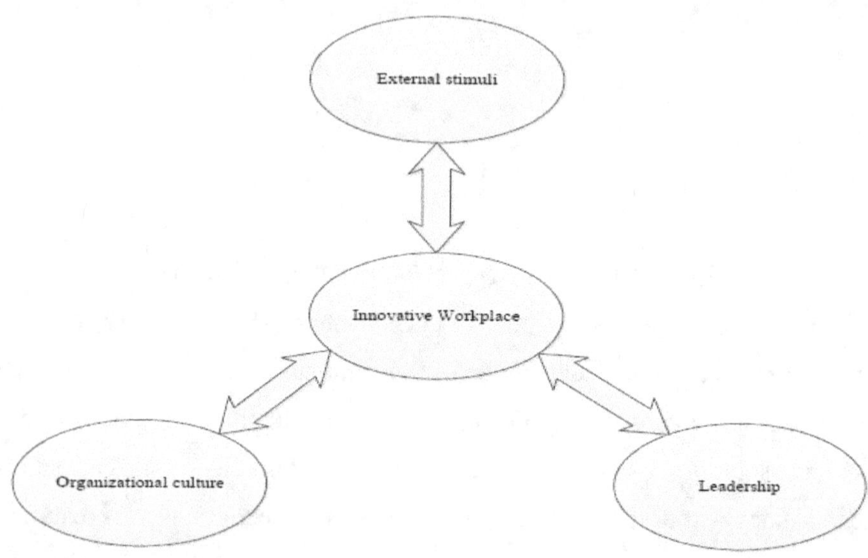

Model of Innovative workplace design

Implications and Outcomes of the Research Questions

The data analysis from the research study assisted in answering the research questions and validating the documentation discussed in the literature views. The research questions were developed to address the "what" (i.e., textual) and "how" (i.e., structural) descriptive components of the leadership effect on innovative culture phenomenon, which are embodied in RQ1 and RQ2. Subsequent questions RQ3 and RQ4 were designed to further elucidate the effects of the phenomenon and to add additional context for the collective intentionality present in the organizational culture (Baxter & Jack, 2008; Nenon, 2012; Petty, Thomson, & Stew, 2012; Schwandt, 2007). The following are the outcomes for the research questions:

RQ1. Define the organizational culture here at the county and what are the key components and change opportunities?

The results of the study indicated most participants noted the existence of multiple cultures at the county because of the variety of business lines and customers that each area served. This viewpoint was consistent in all management levels are articulated in much the same manner according to leadership risk aversion in each setting. Participants noted that each business line and its leaders had different tolerances for risk based on historical and programmatic components. For example, several study participants noted pressure to conform to external imposed guidelines of funding as the defining characteristic of an area's ability to provide innovative solution or service delivery mechanism to address constituent need.

This compliance centered culture was more prevalent in business support functional areas (e.g., finance or HR) as opposed to direct service areas (e.g., taxpayer services, client services, or corrections). The transactional orientation of programmatic operations, such as client intake and eligibility determination, also leaned heavily on compliance and to what one participant described as "widget-minded." This finding is consistent with the knowledge intensive classification models (i.e., integration, collaboration, transaction, and expert) articulated in Davenport, 2005, which differentiates the type of work activities (e.g., routine, expert, systematic, or improvisational) knowledge workers execute in the course of a day.

Transactional activities that must conform to rigid external guidelines (e.g., federal, state, or local regulations) provide limited opportunity to deploy innovative service delivery mechanism and retain operational transparency with regulatory entities. The innovative options increase dependent on work activities inherent in the remaining models. An example of this would be at the program manager or director level (e.g., integrative or collaborative) where the structure of a service delivery system might be designed in such a way as to incorporate multiple functional components (internal and external) to achieve an organizational strategy.

RQ2. What are key leadership components you feel are necessary to promote innovation change, workflow collaboration, and knowledge sharing?

The factors county knowledge workers perceived as enablers for their acceptance of organizational changes were effective communication, clearly articulated and consistent goals from management, clear responsibilities and expectations from management, flexibility in change implementation, a healthy working environment, proper training, teamwork, and an acceptable system of personal rewards and incentives. The results of the study supported the belief that participants are willing to be guided by leaders to understand and embrace their change responsibilities and functions through identification of personal and organizational advantages (i.e., short versus long term value dimension).

Another human-centric activity involves relationship building and the development of transactional trust as a means of addressing complex knowledge worker interactions. The data results indicated that leaders may need to create a suitable and healthy working environment based on effective communication, clear goals, high performance expectations, and well-defined organizational objectives. Understanding the human challenges relative to operational team membership is essential to the creation of a knowledge sharing culture and change readiness capabilities provides significant implications for governmental enterprises. Assimilation to different working cultures is the key component for the operational success for the entire organization (Brake, 2008; Gang, Shu-tao, & Qiang, 2009).

Such assimilation is the means to manage and accommodate cultural differences inherent in a diverse knowledge worker population and serves as a mitigation of the effects of unexpected or adverse events that occur prior, during, and post-transformation of organizational changes. Literature indicates the presence of at least two human centric factors (social ties and knowledge sharing) and the contribution the two factors comprise internal stakeholder collaboration (Gilley, McMillan, & Gilley, 2009: Gumusluoğlu & Ilsev, 2009). The data indicates that human and organizational factors, such as rapport and transaction memory, play a significant role in facilitating effective knowledge worker collaboration and a sense of empowerment (Brake, 2008; Crawford, Hasan, Warne, & Linger, 2009; Gang, Shu-tao, & Qiang, 2009). The importance of the assimilation process and adjusting to the new working environment is the highest concern among employees.

RQ3. Responsive government: What does the term mean relative to operational or intuitional change and how would you know that you have mobilized organizational resources to achieve it?

The findings relative to this question established the context in which the leadership effect on innovation manifest in the organizational unit response to a particular set of constituent needs. The responses to this question was framed as how best to organize county resources to address a resident need and followed along the deployment of specific programmatic functions that benefited residents.

RQ4. What is the appropriate role for external partners and communities of interest in the operation of governmental agency workflows and how they should be structured?

The findings for this research question established the context for how community-based and regulatory body involvement contributes to the restructure of programs and resources to align with the need of the community. The county has a long history of community involvement in the structure of the operational components of the programs offered, and this commitment starts with the elected county board members and in not political party dependent.

Leadership and organizational culture are linked to and inherent to the process of change. According to Kotter (1998), effective leadership is inherent to the development and nurturing of cultures that are adaptive to change. Other authors note that leadership is an emergent and symbiotic reactive process which is responsive to organizational climate and culture (King & Cotterill, 2007; Liu, Siu, & Shi, 2010). Still others have found substantial linkage between leadership participation and the creation of an innovative culture, which serves as a predictor of high performing organization (Bassiti & Ajhoun, 2013; Kira & Van Eijnatten, 2008; Liou & Korosec, 2009).

Two opposing perspectives are persistent in the literature about leader's effect on organizational culture. The functionalist perspective posits the notion that leaders architect culture change either through substantive or visible organizational actions (e.g., leadership vision) or through the symbolic roles (e.g., early adopters or change agent) they occupy in the enterprise (Jonsdottir, 2013; Sarros & Cooper, 2008; Liu, Siu, & Shi, 2010). Conversely, the anthropological viewpoint challenges the validity of a leader's ability to create or shape culture because those leaders are a product of organizational culture, as opposed to apart from it (i.e., passive participant).

The body of research seems tilted toward the functionalist perspective, which positions leaders to shape the organization's culture and those organizational managers and executives can make or remake the organizational environment (Sarros & Cooper, 2008; Lipford & Slice, 2007). Jung, Chow, and Wu (2003) advanced the notion that transformational leadership enhances knowledge worker innovation by appealing to intrinsic personal value systems and elevating levels of motivation toward higher performance levels and encouraging employees to think creatively.

Analysis of Study Results

The data analysis reported in Chapter 4 resulted in the emergence of four themes. Each theme originated from the participant's patterns of responses to the interview questions. The four emergent themes were Innovative Workplace, Leadership, External stimuli, and Organizational Culture. The following sections include descriptions of the themes and resultant invariant constituents supported by individual participant responses. A summary of the four themes is presented.

Theme 1: Innovative Workplace

ROWE was cited as an important component of an innovative workplace environment and was thought to an initiative that required a high risk tolerance from county's leadership. This initiative was also supported by the county's commitment to deploying information and communication technologies to allow programmatic services to be less building-centric and more client-centric. The county's commitment to providing holistic services provision prompted a move to position the county's service offerings in the communities where there are the greatest need as opposed to buildings centrally located in downtown offices.

Theme 2: Leadership

Leadership characteristics frequently cited were clear articulation of an organizational vision, setting high performance expectations, expecting excellence from work efforts, trust relationships, and a high risk tolerance. Other characteristics included clear and concise communication vehicles that supported transparent interactive relationship exchanges. Preponderance of these leadership characteristics and qualities served as foundational to the establishment of transactional trust essential for an innovative workplace environment.

Theme 3: External stimuli

As noted in other sections of this book, the organizational culture is predicated on compliance with programmatic guidelines established by state, federal, and local authorities. These guidelines can relate to how programmatic funds are used or what populations are to be served. These guidelines can be established at a national level (e.g., Medicaid or Medicare), state level (e.g., aid to cities and counties), or local (e.g., specific communities).

Theme 4: Organizational Culture

The findings support the notion that multiple cultures exist at the county that follow programmatic or area specific and can follow the orientation of the various leaders. In those areas of direct service provision, there is a strong culture of inclusion and generation of solution based on responsive to need.

Support areas of the county tend to be more compliance-oriented and delivering value to taxpayers.

Implications and Significance of the Findings

The results of the current research study of supervisory knowledge workers at the county are important because the findings of the study provided valuable insights about the perceptions and experiences of 21 management professionals relative to leadership. As well as its effect on fostering an organizational culture that embraces change and promotes innovation as an emergent characteristic of that environment. Developing an understanding of leadership behavior can lead to insights and strategies for deploying tactical responses to the need to create a supportive environment for knowledge workers to collaborate on creative or innovative solutions to operational challenges.

Relative to the current single case research study and the significance of its findings to organizational leadership, Luftman (2008) posited that the issues to retain and engaging knowledge workers requires an enterprise-wide commitment to enhancing team performance. The insights that emerged from the results of the qualitative single case phenomenological study are significant to leadership by contributing to the identified gaps of knowledge through the investigation of the insights and experiences of management knowledge workers relative to the leadership phenomenon and its role in creating a culture of innovation.

The synthesis of the composite textural-structural descriptions revealed an influential relationship between organizational work environment, knowledge worker-leadership relationship, external stimuli, and the prevailing organizational culture. An understanding of the underlying relationships might help organizational leaders modify structures and policies of the enterprise in the hopes that such strategies are synergistically congruent with the expectations and value dimensions of knowledge workers inhibiting the governmental fitness landscape.

Recommendations

For Future Research:

Recent research studies indicated the existence of organizational performance issues are related to deficiencies in transactional trust among knowledge workers and manifest in lack of engagement and complacency (Brake,

2008; Lipford & Slice, 2007; Sarros & Cooper, 2008). These factors result is frequent turnover of experienced management professionals, reduced opportunities to develop organizational "bench strength', and a lack of innovative problem solving for operational challenges (Bassiti & Ajhoun, 2013; Jonsdottir, 2013; Luftman, 2008; Sarros & Cooper, 2008).

The findings from the current research study provided information on knowledge workers' expectation and satisfaction with leadership, the innovative effects that emerge from the workplace environment, and organizational strategies that might have an effect on worker's morale and task engagement (Agin & Gibson, 2010; Jonsdottir, 2013; Liu, Siu, & Shi, 2010; Jung, Chow, & Wu, 2003). However, this book population sample did not include Gen Y knowledge workers, which could have produced different study results relative to and across all value dimensions. For example, book participants noted that new hires to the County bring a new work ethic to organization which is likely to proliferate as these members move into the management ranks (Pratt, 2010; Spangenburg, 2014). It recommended that future research include Gen Y management knowledge workers and investigate the effect this group might have on value dimensions such as distance to power, uncertainty avoidance, or collectivism versus individualism.

For Operational Management:

Leadership practitioners seeking to implement innovation workplace strategy roadmaps could consider the establishment of supportive work practices that include transparent systems of compensation, employee recruitment and retention, career tracking, promotional policies, and process improvement. The order of implementation for these systems is critical in that a process improvement program might have limited success if transactional trust has not been established through work practices that support transparency and workplace equity. Prompting innovation in the workplace is complicated if the reward structure does not enhance knowledge worker long-term value dimension orientation and desire-belief structure. Work practices that satisfy workers conditions of satisfaction for employment provides the foundation for capturing and managing organizational knowledge (i.e., tacit and explicit).

Conclusion

The role of government in the lives of citizens will in most respects continue unchanged for the foreseeable future because it provides services that cannot be allocated totally to the private section. Services such as child protection, services for the homeless, and law enforcement are societal goods that must be delivered in a transparent manner. The manner in which those services are delivered has been the subject of much internal and external scrutiny regarding service efficacy. The size and scope of government is a hotly debated political topic that enjoys significant attention during election season. Leaders in the public arena must be cognizant of the need not only to respond to constituent need for services, but also to structure those responses in a cost-efficient and timely manner.

To that end, the leadership of governmental agencies must engage its knowledge workforce in the development of solutions that are innovative and address the supply and demand needs of constituents. To ensure knowledge worker engagement requires leadership attention to the work systems that support these workers. These work systems include workplace policies and practices that engender transactional trust that facilitates the knowledge sharing, collaboration, and cooperation critical to the innovation creation process. Workplaces that are worker-centric and transparent foster an organizational culture that values its workers produce an environment that is inclusive and supportive of work efforts (Armstrong, Flood, Guthrie, Liu, MacCurtain, & Mkamwa, 2010; Lowe & Locke, 2008).

Most governmental organizations are engaged in a continual journey to provide services to constituents in a cost-efficient and outcome-effective manner. These enterprises must also respond to environmental challenges and opportunities perpetuated by change events in its fitness landscape (ecosystem) (Teisman & Klijn, 2008). Literature supports the theory that knowledge worker engagement is critical to the development of innovative and creative solutions to address these ecosystem disruptions (Danylkiv, 2013; Mischen & Jackson, 2008; Nath, 2011; Neves, 2009). Achieving optimal engagement requires leadership to create the conditions that foster a work environment, culture, and climate that provides workers with the work systems that allow the free flow of information and collaboration essential to the innovative process.

Such work systems provide the framework for high performing teams that focus on metrics driven actions, targeted process improvement, capability building, and organizational learning (Armstrong, Flood, Guthrie, Liu, MacCurtain, & Mkamwa, 2010; Jonsdottir, 2013). Several authors suggest that such an environment is only possible through a reinventing of government (Osborne & Gaebler, 1992; Wong, 2010; Yoon & Kuchinke, 2005). This thinking is consistent with authors suggesting a move to post bureaucratic like structure that promote more of an entrepreneurial orientation that departs from the structure inherent since the industrial era. One vehicle that could promote such a move is embedded in the development of a TREK leadership mindset that embodies a set of core values that fit the prevailing organizational culture's value dimensions (Brake, 2008; Hofstede & Minkov, 2010; Neves, 2009).

Transparency would be at the core of this mindset and would encompass internal and external transactions. Internally, this transparency dimension establishes a performance expectation that knowledge workers will engage in transactions in which the whole of interactions are understood, communicated, and consistent with established organizational norms (Page & Vella-Brodrick, 2009; Steinhoff & Posner, 2010). This transparency is an essential leadership competence.

Reliability establishes a framework for conducting work efforts or processes that is based on evidence-based practices reviewed regularly to ensure that optimal standards are deployed to produce predictable workflow outcomes (Brake, 2008). Equity in work systems reflects dependable communication, fair treatment, and reasonable vehicles for reward and recognition of work efforts, which include issues such as diversity, training, and retention strategies (Beauregard, 2011; Jonsdottir, 2013; Robert, Dennis & Hung, 2009). Knowledge management strategies are a critical activity for any organization in that the explicit and tacit worker knowledge must be optimized to assist in the production of organizational competitive advantage and cultural narrative (Agin & Gibson, 2010; Davenport, 2005; Van Mierlo, Rutte, Vermunt, Kompier, & Doorewaard, 2007).

The traditional model for government resembles an Industrial-era bureaucratic design that was intended to minimize inept patronage type structures (Burnes, 2009; Grey & Garsten, 2001). However, the dynamic forces of the prevailing environment relative to global competitiveness, instantaneous communication, knowledge-centric economies, and target-marketing can result in pedestrian performance, inflexible processes, and a fixation on command and control (Carlisle & McMillan, 2006; Desouza & Lin, 2011).

The potential gains that are achievable through the deployment of information and communication technology to build e-government appliances make public services accessible online. The deployment of technology to facilitate the delivery of governmental services provides opportunities to create a form of entrepreneurial government (Dawes, 2008; Osborne & Gaebler, 1992)

The globalization pace dictates the need for a update to the existing model of government inspired by the notion of "entrepreneurial government", which describes an entity that is adaptive to change, responsive to constituents, cost-efficient, and outcome effective (Dovifat, Brüggemeier, & Lenk, 2007). A governmental agency such as this should be able to produce high quality service delivery, be led by persuasion and incentives as opposed to command, and be entrepreneurial in its operational approach.

The current operational environment necessitates that leaders of governmental entities be more flexible and adaptable, be sensitive to constituent needs, give workers a sense of mission and ownership, and empowering citizens, while providing value-added services that increasingly those citizens have come to expect and demand (Osborne & Gaebler, 1992; Robichau, 2011).

Traditional bureaucracies have cultivated tendencies in people to defend their organizational position, resist change, enhance organizational authorities, enlarge their sphere of influence and control, encourage or defend initiatives without regard to relevance to present operational settings, and protection of the status quo (Gilley, McMillan, & Gilley, 2009; Liu, Siu, & Shi, 2010; Pollitt, 2009). Conversely, entrepreneurial or post-bureaucratic government produces more cost-efficient and outcome-effective models of managing organizational ecosystems (Ostroff, 2006; Persson & Goldkuhl, 2010; Pollitt, 2009). Such a government model acknowledges the importance of discarding outdated and inappropriate programs and processes (Gilley, McMillan, & Gilley, 2009; Gumusluoğlu & Ilsev, 2009).

Post-bureaucratic organizations encourage executing timely and appropriate action. It is an entity that is creative and innovative. It is business-oriented and seeks external sourcing when it makes pragmatic sense, or when private operators can offer similar levels of service more effectively. It also provides an operational space for new ventures and revenue-generating operations. Post-bureaucratic enterprises are customer-focused, adopt transparent performance metrics, and rewards meritorious actions (Jamrog, Vickers, & Bear, 2006). It is a governmental structure that embraces change and challenges. In summary, an entrepreneurial or post-bureaucratic government enhances the ability to continually improve its resource utilization in the most comprehensive context or meaning (Hornung, Rousseau, & Glaser, 2008; Osborne & Gaebler, 1992; Pollitt, 2009).

Chapter 6

Case Study Epilogue

This book would not be complete without a revisit to the case subject of the dissertation research which contributed to a substantial amount of data analysis and conclusions. The case study subject is the largest county in Minnesota which has Minneapolis as its county seat. The Minneapolis/St. Paul (aka Twin Cities) metro area is comprised of seven counties which made the research results comparable and generalizability to similarly situations metro areas assuming alignment to population and ethnic density. The crux of the research was to analyze the factors that generate positive workforce interactions and provide the highest return to its resident constituents and operational ecosystem. Using a complex adaptive system (CAS) theory approach, the data could be arranged and stratified by each level of the bureaucracy. The emergent themes could then be summarized as being the prevailing anthropological equivalent of the county culture. As mentioned in previous chapters, a CAS strategy is useful in that organizations can resemble bio-organisms that exist in a defined ecosystem and structures its environmental response behaviors based on external and internal actor's interactions. Public entities are not unique in that regard, the same could be said for private sector organizations as well, albeit with different actors. The most dynamic of those actors in the private sector is the shareholder group. Defining the shareholders in the private sector is much easier because ownership rights are defined, documented and subject to litigation for breaches in shareholder value return expectations. Public sector entities can include shareholders from both sectors because return value segregation is not inherent in a free society. For example, if a road is built or light rail is provided as a public utility, any sector and its members become stakeholders who can make use of that good or service.

Having said that, how is it possible to provide maximum value return that conform to "stakeholders" expectations? Stakeholders in the context of public sector ecosystem actors serves to centralize groups of competing needs which can cause disruptions and operational paradigms shifts. Within these stakeholder groups there are any number of competing interests. For example, urban and rural value expectations will not always align. Generally, these competing interest groups will determine a range in which they will be satisfied in terms of value return. These conditions of satisfaction will be communicated to representatives of those groups during discussion and decision making amongst the governance mechanisms established to discharge the business matters of the collective ecosystem. Political elections provide some of that range determination and the focus of how the ecosystem's resources will be deployed. The dynamics of the political process is fascinating and is worthy of its own writings, but suffice it to say, each political actor will favor a set of policies that favor social needs as opposed to corporate needs.

If we were to posit a group concept of the value proposition, a stakeholder group might seek operational structures that produce the kind of value returns it desires, and possess a willingness to provide innovative and cost-effective processes that increase stakeholder's value return. If you favor roads and bridges over food stamps funding, you'll want your ecosystem partner to focus on those outcomes. If on the other hand you tend to favor socially responsible programs that provide physical and emotional benefits, your concept of return on investment will be vastly different. In terms of public institutions, ecosystem stakeholders elect representatives to school boards, city councils, commissioners, regents and state houses in order to shape the operational agenda for a particular ecosystem segment. These elected officials collectively formulate the vision for their respective public institution according to whatever promises that have been made to their constituents. To ensure that elected officials adhere to the wishes of their constituent groups, there can be additional oversight bodies that are made up of permanent or temporary members of those groups. These oversight groups interact regularly with their representative in formal or informal gatherings (e.g., town hall meetings) in which interested members can voice their support or concern for the actions of that representative.

While these election events can be useful for developing the high level operational vision for that segment, the actual work of these institutions is done by some members of the constituent themselves. Thus, becoming both a stakeholder and support staff in the same ecosystem segment. As noted in previous chapters, CAS can be used to explain how these various ecosystem members can occupy both roles and not be in conflict. For example, an ecosystem actor can vote for a particular set of objectives, participate in the tactic plan to achieve the vison, and help execute those plans. As long as no one role causes an imbalance such that it creates a disequilibrium in the ecosystem as a whole. The 2016 presidential election provides an example of such an imbalance. The thought being that a group of actors vote for a candidate that espouses all of the group's core attitudes and beliefs, despite seeming to be a polar opposite of that group's defined values. Or put another way, you can love the message contained in a vision but hate the messenger. Those who voted for Trump did so because he told them exactly what they wanted to hear and allowed some to express viewpoints that were not in step with the boarder community and its standards. The Alabama senatorial election provides another example of this phenomenon in that Roy Moore was a clearly flawed person, but he espoused all of the closely held attitudes and beliefs of a segment of the electoral ecosystem. The Book of Judges in the Old Testament bible also illustrates this phenomenon in that God used people of questionable character to rule over the tribes of Israel. Samson was such a character because of his reported womanizing behavior and frequent visits to carnal establishments. He would not have survived today's 24-hour news media scrutiny. History is replete with other such examples of ecosystem members tapping into the group physic and embodying that group's vision (i.e., cultural warrior) for their segment of the world. What does all of this mean in the current context of this writing? As noted in previous chapters, the concept of leadership is rooted in most of the traditional and contemporary literature. The importance of this role is in its constituent-facing and interfacing role in a defined ecosystem, because the leader embodies the core beliefs and value proposition. Key characteristics of such leadership are scholarship, which is embodied by a thirst for lifelong learning; practice, which encourages advances in social and workplace contribution; and the ability to exert positive influence through empathetic leadership activities. These qualities are critical because the expectation is that the leader will define, communicate, articulate and execute a vision that can be embraced by members of their organization or ecosystem segment.

Having a clearly articulated organizational vision helps establish the operational framework for an entity's workflows and provides the cornerstone that can serve as a rallying point for all organizational members. The vision also provides a validation mechanism by which operational workflows can be evaluated in terms of practicality and value creation. Leaders are the keepers of the vision and seek to balance the possible with the probably course of events that contribute to achieving the organizational mission. Leaders must also inspire others to behave in a manner that allows work to be performed that furthers the organizational goals and return value to the ecosystem stakeholders. The willingness to be influenced to produce value for stakeholders has been the subject of much debate and strategy development. As noted in prior chapters, those charged with ecosystem workflow execution do so according to personal belief theory. Belief theory suggests that one's willingness to be sycophantic to others is in direct relationship to that person's belief that a beneficial good will be achieved in a defined course of action. This willingness can also be defined by one's commitment to the goals of an organization and the level of intensity they will put inject into their defined workflow responsibilities. The workflow intensity can also be in conflict with other factors (e.g., family and friends) that vie for a worker's time. Achieving a work life balance follows this concept in that there is a finite amount of external pain one is willing to endure to achieve personal goals relative to one's well-being.

Understanding this dynamic is particularly important to worker productivity and a worker's willingness to contribute to organizational goals in a meaningful way. Transactional trust is a key issue to review in this context. As noted in previous chapters, a positive level of trust is only achieved when there is transparency in the exchange relationship (e.g., terms and conditions of employment). If there is a question of worker fairness and it is not resolved in a manner that is above reproach, the employment relationship can be damaged. This can also result in a lack of employee engagement in the achievement of organizational goals and objectives. In some industries, such disengagement can mean lower quality goods produced and loss of consumer market share. In a human services context, lack of employee engagement can result in loss of life. Another factor in achieving transactional trust and worker engagement is having clearly defined workflow roles that align with bona fide job qualifications. Aligning workflow roles with worker qualifications (i.e., Resource-based Management Theory) helps establish technical competency in workplace interactions because those workers process the baseline knowledge needed to discharge their duties. Baseline knowledge can be evidenced by academic achievement in a field of study relating to a position in question. In the case study county, this baseline knowledge was not always apparent in middle management worker selection. For example, one might expect that the Chief Information Officer (CIO) in an organization would have academic credentials in an information technology field of study, which is not the case in the county. That person has a public administration background. Since government agencies don't share the private sector organizational hierarchy, CIO is more of a middle management role. Needless to say, the lack of entry level knowledge in a field can result in errors in judgment in either sector because that person would not be able to establish the vision for technology deployment due to unfamiliarity with the underlying concepts of information and communication technology.

Case in point was a deployment of an enterprise resource planning (ERP) application module to capture information technology worker time spent on the various organizational technology projects. The time reporting project had the current and prior CIOs as its executive sponsors and the final implemented solution was not consistent with the ERP module design specifications that was purchased by the county. This ERP module was designed to interface with Microsoft Project and produce an enterprise view of all technology projects and the resources expended. The final project solution was implemented with a flawed approach to this ERP module in that it used a framework that was configured improperly, which a properly trained technology practitioner would have detected in very short order. The effect of this deployment results in poor utilization of an expensive resource that was purchased with taxpayer dollars and intense manual labor to provide usable information.

This issue was also noted in the Case Family Report as an internal systems problem. Case Family Programs, a national review/compliance consultant, requested that the technology department to produce a custom report of child and family operations in an effort to evaluate the effectiveness of that department. What was produced for the investigators did not meet their expectations and they noted that the report was unusable because of its poor structure and convoluted conclusions. The investigators noted that there were significant issues with the county's data operations and recommended changes to the manner is which data is gathered, reported and stored.

These issues noted above can be directly attributed to a lack of middle management expertise and training in the job classifications that they occupy. One might expect that quality control procedures would have been followed so that such problems would be addressed in the normal course of a properly trained manager's duties. Most of the middle managers at the county came up through the ranks of the organizations and occupied roles other than their current roles. In many cases, people with technical proficiency in one role were promoted to management because of tenue in those technical roles. In other cases, staff without entry level qualifications were promoted to management positions within other job classifications, such as social worker promoted into technology management positions without obtaining the requisite technology training. This type of promotion was commonplace at the county and contributes to a lack of fairness shared by longer term county employees. Past and more recent employee surveys validate this assertion and consistently surfaces as a significant organizational problem. This type of promotion based on tenure and manager sycophantic favor over technical competency and academic training can contribute to multiple workflow wastes and operational inefficiencies. The manager favoritism issue is also problematic in that it establishes a tribal-like culture that pits one group of staff against another because of the fear of retribution. This fear instance was validated during the fieldwork portion of the Case Family Program engagement where investigators were brought in to assess the county's child and family services area. The report delivered by Case Family Program found a significant number of operational problems both in its processes and personnel. The most telling personnel issue was the general uneasiness with the way management interacted with staff and the investigators found that there was fear of retribution from management for delivering adverse results.

Another factor that limits the development of transactional trust involves fairness in the hiring and promotional policies and procedures. If an employee feels that they are being unfairly hindered in either of those fronts, they are less likely to fully engage in the work of the organization. If the hiring and retention policies are seen as unfair, the organization should make every effort to dispel that notion and ensure its employees about how such decisions are made relative to process ordered and discharge. For example, hiring and promotional selection criteria should be clearly communicated to prospective candidates, along with the scoring algorithm used to select the best qualified candidate. In addition to clearly communicated selection criteria, all scoring material should be made available to show how a successful candidate was chosen. There should also be a minimally onerous internal process that allows employees to determine for themselves, the fairness of the selection of a particular person. This can occur with an employee inquiry to the human resource department to "show their work" when it came to that selection. Such a process might start with the advancement of a concern that a selected candidate was less qualified than others that may have been in the candidate pool. Human resources would review the selection material and communicate the scoring and evaluation used to select that candidate. If the employee agrees, problem solved. If not, a second step could be a meeting with the hiring supervisor to discuss any disputed points in the evaluation and hiring process. If there is still no resolution to the employee's concern, a discussion could occur at the one or two levels above the hiring supervisor to align the criteria that was used to select that person. Litigation could occur if needed after that 3rd step. In that manner, the employee concerns would be handled internally in most cases. This is not the case at the county.

In a recent case at the county, a charge of employment and promotional discrimination was referred to an external attorney for investigation in the second step, as opposed to going through an internal process to evaluate the claim using internal county staff. The first step was lodging the complaint to staff not trained in human resources and was for the most part were charged with recording the issue and referring to the internal audit department. From there the complaint went directly to an external lawyer for investigation. The issue with engaging an external resource is that such a resource would not be aware of the idiosyncratic nature or culture of the organization. That resource would also not be aware of prevailing issues that have historical underpinning. The use of an external resource would also send the signal that an adversary relationship exists between the employee and the organization, which damages transactional trust. There are instances where external resources are critical to truth finding, but their use should be done relative to adherence to operational best practices. In most cases, employees raise issues because on concerns about the organization because they see value in working there, but want to be treated fairly. They use internal processes as a means to effect changes or seek validation for some action the organization has taken. Using a step internal complaint process allows employees to air grievances at various levels of the organization and obtain a fully articulated response to their concerns. This kind of approach also demonstrates a level of organizational empathy to the concerns of their employees, which is turn create a positive employment exchange transaction. Creating a workplace that provides a positive sense of employee well-being will help workers to engage in creative and innovative activities designed to achieve organizational goals and objectives.

As noted in previous chapters, innovation is a direct byproduct of an engaged and motivated workforce. Transactional trust is a key component of building employee relationships from which mutual benefits are achieved. Absence that trust, workers will focus more on achieving their own short and long-term goals, with little regard to how those goals align with the organization. In many cases, the work products that are generated from those work processes will be of lesser quality and quantity. Leadership is not only about establishing the vision, but to also determine the most appropriate operational strategy to achieve that vision. Understanding the operational ecosystem, its actor sub-systems behavior and alignment strategies is most often a function of properly trained middle management. Conventional wisdom and extensive literature indicate that the work of any organization is done on the front line, which make middle management staffing critical to overall success. To that end, leaders must ensure that systems (e.g., TREK©) are in place to provide a framework for achieving organizational success and a fully engaged and motivated workforce. The TREK© model advances transparency, reliable systems, equity, and knowledge transfer as the hallmark of an innovative and creative workforce that embraces the challenges of ever-changing ecosystems. In order to improve the operational effectiveness of our public institutions it is incumbent of the relevant ecosystem actors to demand adherence to the fairness doctrines embodied in a sound approach engaging knowledge worker to produce the best work possible to benefit all ecosystem goals and objectives. Not doing so would be inconsistent with closely held values and beliefs of an informed society.

References

Agin, E., & Gibson, T. (2010). Developing an innovative culture. *American Society for Training & Development, 64*(7), 52-55.

Ailon, G. (2008). Mirror, mirror on the wall: Culture's consequences in a value test of its own design. *Academy of Management Review, 33,* 885-904.

Alaa, G. (2009). Derivation of factors facilitating organizational emergence based on complex adaptive systems and social autopoiesis theories. *Emergence: Complexity & Organization, 11,* 19-34

Amabile, T. M., & Kramer, S. J. (2011). The Power of Small Wins. *Harvard Business Review, 89*(5), 70-80.

Amblard, F. (2007). Artificial Life Special Issue on Visualization for Complex Adaptive Systems. [Book Review]. *Journal of Artificial Societies & Social Simulation, 10*(1), 11-11.

Antonelli, G. (2013). The local innovation networks: An explorative study of success cluster. The Business Review, Cambridge, 21(2), 205-211. Retrieved from http://search.proquest.com/docview/1465226249?accountid=458

Armstrong, C., Flood, P. C., Guthrie, J. P., Liu, W., MacCurtain, S., & Mkamwa, T. (2010). The impact of diversity and equality management on firm performance: Beyond high performance work systems. *Human Resource Management, 49*(6), 977-998. doi:10.1002/hrm.20391

Arena, M. J. (2009). Understanding large group intervention processes: A complexity theory perspective. *Organization Development Journal, 27,* 49-64.

Ashkenas, R., Ulrich, D., Jick, T., & Kerr, S. (2002). The boundaryless organization: Breaking the chains of organizational structure. San Francisco, CA, Jossey-Bass.

Aydinoglu, A. U. (2010). Scientific collaborations as complex adaptive systems. *Emergence: Complexity & Organization, 12*(4), 15-29.

Banutu-Gomez, M. B., & Banutu-Gomez, S. M. T. (2007). Leadership and organizational change in a competitive environment. *Business Renaissance Quarterly, 2*(2), 69-90.

Barcan, L. (2009). Current issues on change management in public organizations. *Young Economists Journal/Revista Tinerilor Economisti, 7*(13), 71-74.

Bassiti, L. E., & Ajhoun, R. (2013). Toward an innovation management framework: A life-cycle model with an idea management focus. International Journal of Innovation, Management and Technology, 4(6), 551. doi:http://dx.doi.org/10.7763/IJIMT.2013.V4.460

Baxter, P., & Jack, S. (2008, December). Qualitative Case Study Methodology: Study Design and Implementation for Novice Researchers. The Qualitative Report, 13(4), 544-559.

Beauregard, T. (2011). Direct and Indirect Links between Organizational Work-Home Culture and Employee Well-being. *British Journal of Management, 22*(2), 218-237. doi:10.1111/j.1467-8551.2010.00723.x

Bellamy, C. (2010). Responding to Crises in the Modern Infrastructure. Policy Lessons from Y2K - by Kevin F. Quigley. [Book Review]. *Public Administration, 88*(1), 275-276. doi: 10.1111/j.1467-9299.2010.01818_5.x

Berman, S., & Korsten, P. (2014). Leading in the connected era. Strategy & Leadership, 42(1), 37-46. doi:http://dx.doi.org/10.1108/SL-10-2013-0078

Bhattacherjee, A. (2012). Social Science Research: Principles, Methods, and Practices (2nd Ed.). Tampa, Florida: Creative Commons Attribution-NonCommercial-ShareAlike 3.0 Unported License

Bloch, D. P. (2005). Complexity, Chaos, and Nonlinear Dynamics: A New Perspective on Career Development Theory. [Article]. *Career Development Quarterly, 53*(3), 194.

Boden, R., Cox, D., & Nedeva, M. (2006). The appliance of science? New public management and strategic change. [Article]. *Technology Analysis & Strategic Management, 18*(2), 125-141. doi: 10.1080/09537320600623941

Bovaird, T. (2008). Emergent strategic management and planning mechanisms in complex adaptive systems. *Public Management Review, 10*, 319-340. doi:10.1080/14719030802002741

Boyd, N. (2009). Implementing large-scale Organization Development and

Change in the States. [Article]. *Public Administration Quarterly, 33*(2), 233-269.

Brake, T. (2008). *Where in the world is my team? Making a success of your virtual global workplace.* San Francisco, CA: Jossey-Bass.

Brcar, F., & Lah, S. (2011). Innovation management and an innovative ideas system. Organizacija, 44(1), 3. doi:http://dx.doi.org/10.2478/v10051-011-0001-1

Burnes, B. (2009). Reflections: Ethics and Organizational Change - Time for a Return to Lewinian Values. [Article]. *Journal of Change Management, 9*(4), 359-381. doi: 10.1080/14697010903360558

Butler, M. J. R., & Allen, P. M. (2008). Understanding policy implementation processes as self-organizing systems. *Public Management Review, 10*, 421-440.

Calderón-Ruiz, G., & Sepúlveda, M. (2011). Discovering the source of failures. [Article]. *Industrial Engineer: IE, 43*(3), 46-50.

Carlisle, Y., & McMillan, E. (2006). Innovation in organizations from a complex adaptive systems perspective. *Emergence: Complexity & Organization, 8*, 2-9.

Caudle, S. L. (1988). Federal information resources management after the Paperwork Reduction Act. *Public Administration Review, 48*, 790-799.

Chorba, K. (2011). A review of qualitative research: Studying how things work. The Qualitative Report, 16(4), 1136-1140. Retrieved from http://search.proquest.com/docview/877886014?accountid=458

Crawford, K., Hasan, H., Warne, L., & Linger, H. (2009). From traditional knowledge management in hierarchical organizations to a network centric paradigm for a changing world. *Emergence: Complexity & Organization, 11*, 1-18.

Creswell, J. W. (2007). *Qualitative Inquiry & Research Design* (2nd Ed.). Thousand Oaks, CA: Sage Publications, Inc.

Danylkiv, K. P. (2013). Theoretical and Methodological Aspects of the Essence of Innovation in the Context of Modern Approaches. International Journal of Organizational Innovation (Online), 6(2), 26-33. Retrieved from http://search.proquest.com/docview/1446441218?accountid=458

Davenport, T. (2005). Thinking for a living: How to Get Better Performances and Results from Knowledge Workers, Harvard Business Review Press

Dawes, S. S. (2008). The evolution and continuing challenges of e-governance. *Public Administration Review, 68,* S86-S102. doi:10.1111/j.1540-6210.2008.00981.x

deLeon, P., & Varda, D. M. (2009). Toward a Theory of Collaborative Policy Networks: Identifying Structural Tendencies. [Article]. *Policy Studies Journal, 37*(1), 59-74. doi: 10.1111/j.1541-0072.2008.00295.x

Desouza, K. C., & Lin, Y. (2011). Towards evidence-driven policy design: Complex adaptive systems and computational modeling. *Innovation Journal, 16,* 1-19.

DiCicco-Bloom, B., & Crabtree, B. F. (2006). The qualitative research interview.
Medical Education, 40(4), 314-321. Retrieved March 9, 2010, from EBSCOHost
database.

Dovifat, A., Brüggemeier, M., & Lenk, K. (2007). The "model of micropolitical arenas": A framework to understand the innovation process of e-government-projects. *Information Polity: The International Journal of Government & Democracy in the Information Age, 12*(3), 127-138.

Ford, R. (2008). Complex adaptive systems and improvisation theory: Toward framing a model to enable continuous change. *Journal of Change Management, 8,* 173-198. doi:10.1080/14697010802567543

Foxon, T. J., Reed, M. S., & Stringer, L. C. (2009). Governing long-term social–ecological change: what can the adaptive management and transition management approaches learn from each other? [Article]. *Environmental Policy & Governance, 19*(1), 3-20. doi: 10.1002/eet.496

Gang, Y., Shu-tao, Y. A. N., & Qiang, L. I. U. (2009). A study on the rising of service-oriented government. [Article]. *Journal of US-China Public Administration, 6*(7), 8-16.

Gardner, P. J. (2009). Organizational change: All we want is better projects-why so difficult? *AACE International Transactions, 3,* 1-25.

Garg, A. X., Adhikari, N. K. J., McDonald, H., Rosas-Arellano, M. P., Devereaux, P. J., Beyene, J., et al. (2005). Effects of Computerized Clinical Decision Support Systems on Practitioner Performance and Patient

Outcomes A Systematic Review. *Journal of American Medical Association, 293*(10), 1223-1238.

Gilley, A., McMillan, H. S., & Gilley, J. W. (2009). Organizational Change and Characteristics of Leadership Effectiveness. *Journal of Leadership & Organizational Studies, 16*(1), 38-47.

Graetz, F., & Smith, A. C. T. (2009). Duality theory and organizing forms in change management. *Journal of Change Management, 9*, 9-25. doi:10.1080/14697010902727146

Graml, T., Bracht, R., & Spies, M. (2008). Patterns of business rules to enable agile business processes. [Article]. *Enterprise Information Systems, 2*(4), 385-402. doi: 10.1080/17517570802245441

Grey, C., & Garsten, C. (2001). Trust, control, and the post-bureaucracy. *Organization Studies, 22*, 229-250.

Gumusluoğlu, L., & Ilsev, A. (2009). Transformational leadership and organizational innovation: The roles of internal and external support for innovation. *Journal of Product Innovation Management, 26*, 264-277. doi:10.1111/j.1540-5885.2009.00657

Haynes, P. (2008). Complexity Theory and Evaluation in Public Management. [Article]. *Public Management Review, 10*(3), 401-419. doi: 10.1080/14719030802002766

Hock, D. H. (1995). The chaordic organization: Out of control and into order. *World Business Academy Perspectives, 9*, 1-9.

Hofstede, G., & Minkov, M. (2010). Long- versus short-term orientation: new perspectives. *Asia Pacific Business Review 16*(4), 493-504. doi:10.1080/13602381003637609

Hornung, S., Rousseau, D. M., & Glaser, J. (2008). Creating flexible work arrangements through idiosyncratic deals. *Journal of Applied Psychology, 93*(3), 655-664. doi: 10.1037/0021-9010.93.3.655

Hovenga, E. J. S., Kidd, M. R., Garde, S., & Hullin Lucay Cossio, C. (2010). Change management: An overview. *Studies in Health Technology & Informatics, 151*, 404-412.

Ifinedo, P., & Nahar, N. (2007). ERP systems success: an empirical analysis of how two organizational stakeholder groups prioritize and evaluate relevant measures. *Enterprise Information Systems, 1*, 25-48.

Janson, K. R., & Scheiner, J. H. (2007). Compliance Costs in the Second Year of Sarbanes-Oxley: The Evidence from Bank Audit Fees. [Article]. *Bank Accounting & Finance (08943958), 20*(2), 10-14.

Jamrog, J., Vickers, M., & Bear, D. (2006). Building and Sustaining a Culture that Supports Innovation. [Article]. *Human Resource Planning, 29*(3), 9-19.

Jones, L. R., & McCaffery, J. L. (2010). Performance Budgeting in the U.S. Federal Government: History, Status and Future Implications. [Article]. *Public Finance & Management, 10*(3), 482-523.

Jones, R. A., Jimmieson, N. L., & Griffiths, A. (2005). The impact of organizational culture and reshaping capabilities on change implementation success: The mediating role of readiness for change. *Journal of Management Studies, 42*, 361-386. doi:10.1111/j.1467-6486.2005.00500.x

Jonsdottir, I. J. (2013). Manager's tales about developmental projects: What makes a difference when leading innovation in public sector services? International Journal of Business and Social Science, 4(13) Retrieved from http://search.proquest.com/docview/1462439374?accountid=458

Jun, J. S. (2009). The limits of post-new public management and beyond [Book review]. *Public Administration Review, 69*, 161-165. doi:10.1111/j.1540-6210.2008.01960.x

Karp, T., & Helgø, T. I. (2008). From change management to change leadership: Embracing chaotic change in public service organizations. *Journal of Change Management, 8*, 85-96. doi:10.1080/14697010801937648

King, S., & Cotterill, S. (2007). Transformational Government? The role of information technology in delivering citizen-centric local public services. [Article]. *Local Government Studies, 33*(3), 333-354. doi: 10.1080/03003930701289430

Kira, M., & Van Eijnatten, F. M. (2008). Socially sustainable work organizations: A chaordic systems approach. *Systems Research and Behavioral Science, 25*, 743-756.

Koontz, L. D. (2005). Paperwork Reduction Act: New approach may be needed to reduce government burden on public (GAO-05-424). Washington, DC: U.S. Government Accountability Office.

Koontz, L. D. (2006). Paperwork Reduction Act: Increase in estimated burden hours highlights need for new approach (GAO-06-974T). Washington, DC: U.S. Government Accountability Office.

Kotter, J. P., & Schlesinger, L. A. (2008). Choosing Strategies for Change. [Article]. *Harvard Business Review, 86*(7/8), 130-139.

Krane, D. (2008). Can the "courthouse gang" go modern?: Lessons from the adoption of performance-based management by county governments. *Public Performance & Management Review, 31,* 387-406

Leedy, P. D., & Ormrod, J. E. (2010). Practical research: Planning and design (9th Ed.). Upper Saddle River, NJ: Prentice Hall.

Letzring, T. D., & Snow, M. S. (2011). Mental health practitioners and HIPAA. *International Journal of Play Therapy, 20*(3), 153-164. doi: 10.1037/a0023717

Lichtenstein, B. B., Uhl-Bien, M., Marion, R., Seers, A., Orton, J. D., & Schreiber, C. (2006). Complexity leadership theory: An interactive perspective on leading in complex adaptive systems. *Emergence: Complexity & Organization, 8*(4), 2-12.

Liou, K. T., & Korosec, R. (2009). Implementing organizational reform strategies in state governments. *Public Administration Quarterly, 33,* 429-452.

Lipford, J. W., & Slice, J. (2007). Adam Smith's Roles for Government and Contemporary U.S. Government Roles: Is the Welfare State Crowding Out Government's Basic Functions? *Independent Review, 11*(4), 485-501. doi: http://www.independent.org/publications/tir/

Liu, J., Siu, O., & Shi, K. (2010). Transformational Leadership and Employee Well-Being: The Mediating Role of Trust in the Leader and Self-Efficacy. *Applied Psychology: An International Review, 59*(3), 454-479. doi:10.1111/j.1464-0597.2009.00407.x

Long, S., & Spurlock, D. G. (2008). Motivation and Stakeholder Acceptance in Technology-driven Change Management: Implications for the Engineering Manager. [Article]. *Engineering Management Journal, 20*(2), 30-36.

Lowe, A., & Locke, J. (2008). Enterprise resource planning and the post bureaucratic organization. *Information Technology & People, 21,* 375-400.

Lyons, J. B., Swindler, S. D., & Offner, A. (2009). The Impact of Leadership on Change Readiness in the US Military. [Article]. *Journal of Change Management, 9*(4), 459-475. doi: 10.1080/14697010903360665

Mahoney, J. (2010). AFTER KKV: The new methodology of qualitative research. World Politics, 62(1), 120-II. Retrieved from http://search.proquest.com/docview/274387306?accountid=458

Marsh, I. (2008). Instruction to deliver: Tony Blair, *Public Services and the Challenge of Achieving Targets*, by Michael Barber *The Other Invisible Hand, Delivering Public Services through Choice*, by Julian Le Grand. [Book review]. *Australian Journal of Public Administration, 67*, 231-237. doi:10.1111/j.1467-8500.2008.00584_1.x

Marusis, J. (2010). Does Hume hold a dispositional account of belief? *Canadian Journal of Philosophy, 40*, 155-183.

Mettler, S., & Stonecash, J. M. (2008). Government Program Usage and Political Voice. *Social Science Quarterly, 89*(2), 273-293. doi: http://www.blackwellpublishing.com/journal.asp?ref=0038-4941

Mihm, J. C. (2007). Human Capital: Federal Workforce Challenges in the 21st Century: GAO-07-556T. [Article]. *GAO Reports*, 1.

Millican, P. (2009). Hume, Causal Realism, and Causal Science. [Article]. *Mind, 118*(471), 647-712. doi: 10.1093/mind/fzp095

Mischen, P. A., & Jackson, S. K. (2008). Connecting the dots: applying complexity theory, knowledge management and social network analysis to policy implementation. *Public Administration Quarterly, 32*(3), 314-338.

Moulder, E., & O'Neill Jr, R. J. (2009). Citizen Engagement and Local Government Management. [Article]. *National Civic Review, 98*(2), 21-30.

Moustakas, C. (1994). Summary, implications, and outcomes: A Phenomenological Analysis. In Phenomenological research methods. (pp. 155-177). SAGE Publications, Inc. doi: 10.4135/9781412995658.d10

Nan, N. (2011). Capturing bottom-up information technology use processes: A complex adaptive systems model. *MIS Quarterly, 35*, 505-507.

Nath, J. (2011). Workplace Well-Being and Engagement -- Some Inter- Relations and Their Organizational Impacts. *Proceedings of the European Conference on Management, Leadership & Governance*, 313-320.

Nenon, T. (2012). Hussert and the promise of time: Subjectivity in transcendental phenomenology. The Review of Metaphysics, 66(1), 142-144. Retrieved from http://search.proquest.com/docview/1086332460?accountid=458

Neuman, W. L. (2005). Social research methods: Qualitative and quantitative approaches (6th Ed.). Boston, MA: Allyn & Bacon.

Neves, P. (2009). Readiness for Change: Contributions for Employee's Level of Individual Change and Turnover Intentions. [Article]. *Journal of Change Management, 9*(2), 215-231. doi: 10.1080/14697010902879178

Newman, D. (2006). Quick change. The change acceleration process has been used successfully in business all over the world. *Hospitals & Health Networks / AHA*, 80(2), 84. Retrieved from EBSCOhost

OMB Relaxes PRA Rules for Social Media. (2010). [Article]. *Information Management Journal, 44*(4), 12-12.

Osborne, D., & Gaebler, T., (1992), Reinventing Government – How the Entrepreneurial Spirit is Transforming the Public Sector, Prentice Hall Limited,

Ostroff, F. (2006). Change management in government. *Harvard Business Review, 84*(5), 141-147.

Page, K., & Vella-Brodrick, D. (2009). The 'What', 'Why' and 'How' of Employee Well-Being: A New Model. *Social Indicators Research, 90*(3), 441-458. doi:10.1007/s11205-008-9270-3

Pervez, T., Maritz, A., & Waal, A. D. (2014). Innovation and social entrepreneurship at the bottom of the pyramid - A conceptual framework. South African Journal of Economic and Management Sciences, 16(5), 54. Retrieved from http://search.proquest.com/docview/1466124219?accountid=458

Penn, I. A. (1997). Information management legislation in the last quarter of the 20th century: A records management. *Records Management Quarterly, 31*, 3-9.

Persson, A., & Goldkuhl, G. (2010). Government value paradigms: Bureaucracy, new public management, and e-government. *Communications of AIS, 2010*(27), 45-62.

Petty, N. J., Thomson, O. P., & Stew, G. (2012). Ready for a paradigm shift? Part 2: Introducing qualitative research methodologies and methods. Manual Therapy, 17(5), 378-384. doi: http://dx.doi.org/10.1016/j.math.2012.03.004

Plocher, D. (1996). The Paperwork Reduction Act of 1995: A second chance for information resources management. *Government Information Quarterly, 13*, 35.

Polk, J. D. (2011). Lean Six Sigma, Innovation, and the Change Acceleration Process Can Work Together. *Physician Executive, 37*(1), 38-42. Retrieved from EBSCO*host*.

Pollitt, C. (2009). Bureaucracies remember, Post-bureaucratic organizations forget? *Public Administration, 87*, 198-218. doi:10.1111/j.1467-9299.2008.01738.x

Posner, P. L. (2007). The Continuity of Change: Public Budgeting and Finance Reforms over 70 Years. [Article]. *Public Administration Review, 67*(6), 1018-1029. doi: 10.1111/j.1540-6210.2007.00793.x

Powner, D. A. (2004). Federal Chief Information Officers: Responsibilities, Reporting Relationships, Tenure, and Challenges: GAO-04-823 (pp. 1): U.S. Government Accountability Office.

Pratt, M. K. (2010). When Gen Y Runs the show. [Article]. *Computerworld, 44*(16), 25.

Prince, M., Manolis, C., & Tratner, S. (2009). Qualitative analysis and the construction of causal models. Qualitative Market Research, 12(2), 130-152. doi:http://dx.doi.org/10.1108/13522750910948752

Radin, B. A. (1998). The Government Performance and Results Act (GPRA): Hydra-headed monster or flexible management tool? *Public Administration Review, 58*, 307-316.

Relyea, H. C. (2000). Paperwork Reduction Act reauthorization and government information management issues. *Government Information Quarterly, 17*, 367-393

Rethemeyer, R. K. (2009). Making Sense of Collaboration and Governance: Issues and Challenges. [Article]. *Public Performance & Management Review, 32*(4), 565-573. doi: 10.2753/pmr1530-9576320405

Robert, L. P., Dennis, Alan R., & Hung, Y.-T. C. (2009). Individual swift trust and knowledge-based trust in face-to-face and virtual team members. *Journal of Management Information Systems, 26*, 241-279.

Robichau, R. W. (2011). The Mosaic of Governance: Creating a Picture with Definitions, Theories, and Debates (Vol. 39, pp. 113-131): Wiley-Blackwell.

Robinson, O. C. (2014). Sampling in interview-based qualitative research: A theoretical and practical guide. Qualitative Research in Psychology, 11(1), 25-41. doi:http://dx.doi.org/10.1080/14780887.2013.801543

Römer, I. (2012). Nicolas de warren: Husserl and the promise of time. Subjectivity in transcendental phenomenology. Husserl Studies, 28(3), 251-257. doi:http://dx.doi.org/10.1007/s10743-012-9105-6

Rubin, A. (2008). *Practitioner's guide to using research for evidence-based practice*. Hoboken, NJ: John Wiley & Sons, Inc.

Sacheva, S. (2009). Change management for e-governance. *I-Ways, 32*, 109-117.

Sarros, J. C., & Cooper, B. K. (2008). Building a Climate for Innovation through Transformational Leadership and Organizational Culture. *Journal of Leadership & Organizational Studies, 15 Number 2*.

Scherbaum, S., & Dshemuchadse, M. (2008). Making decisions with a continuous mind. *Cognitive, Affective, & Behavioral Neuroscience, 8*, 454-474.

Schönfelder, W. (2011). CAQDAS and Qualitative Syllogism Logic-NVivo 8 and MAXQDA 10 Compared. *Forum: Qualitative Social Research, 12*(1), n/a.

Schwandt, T. A. (2007). *The Sage dictionary of qualitative inquiry* (3rd Ed.). Thousand Oaks, CA: Sage.

Shin, D. (2006). Distributed inter-organizational systems and innovation processes. *Internet Research, 16*(5), 553-572.

Spangenburg, J. M. (2014). The dawn of radical change: A case for leadership. Journal of American Academy of Business, Cambridge, 19(2), 179-185. Retrieved from http://search.proquest.com/docview/1464957288?accountid=458

Sprehe, J. T. (1987). Policy on management of federal information resources. *Journal of the American Society for Information Science, 38*, 30-33.

Stake, R. E. (2010). Qualitative Research: Studying how Things Work: Guilford Press.

Steinhoff, J. C., & Posner, P. L. (2010). Is government turning a new page in accountability, transparency and intergovernmental relations? *Journal of Government Financial Management, 59*, 12-20.

Stewart, T. A. (2006). Growth as a Process. *Harvard Business Review*, 84(6), 60-70. Retrieved from EBSCOhost.

Sutanto, J., Kankanhalli, A., Tay, J., Raman, K. S., & Tan, B. C. Y. (2008). Change Management in Inter-organizational Systems for the Public. [Article]. *Journal of Management Information Systems, 25*(3), 133-175.

Symington, P. (2012). Kant and phenomenology. The Review of Metaphysics, 66(2), 380-382. Retrieved from http://search.proquest.com/docview/1264432997?accountid=458

Symon, G. (2000). Information and communication technologies and the network organization: A critical analysis. *Journal of Occupational & Organizational Psychology, 73*, 389.

Teisman, G. R., & Klijn, E.-H. (2008). Complexity theory and public management. *Public Management Review, 10*, 287-297. doi:10.1080/14719030802002451

Thompson, J. R. (2006). The Federal Civil Service: The Demise of an Institution. [Article]. *Public Administration Review, 66*(4), 496-503. doi:10.1111/j.1540-6210.2006.00609.x

Valerdi, R., Nightingale, D., & Blackburn, C. (2009). Enterprises as systems: Context, boundaries, and practical implications. [Article]. *Information Knowledge Systems Management, 7*(4), 377-399.

Van Mierlo, H., Rutte, C. G., Vermunt, J. K., Kompier, M. A. J., & Doorewaard, J. A. C. M. (2007). A multi-level mediation model of the relationships between team autonomy, individual task design and psychological well-being. [Article]. *Journal of Occupational & Organizational Psychology, 80*(4), 647-664.

Von Der Linn, R. (2009, January 25). Overview of GE's Change Acceleration Process (CAP) [Web log post]. Retrieved from http://bvonderlinn.wordpress.com/2009/01/25/overview-of-ges-change-acceleration-process-cap/

Wagenaar, H. (2007). Governance, Complexity, and Democratic Participation: How Citizens and Public Officials Harness the Complexities of Neighborhood Decline. *The American Review of Public Administration,, 37*(1), 17-50.

Walker, D. M. (2005). 21st Century Challenges: Transforming Government to Meet Current and Emerging Challenges: GAO-05-830T (pp. 1): U.S. Government Accountability Office.

Willis, J. W. (2007). Foundations of qualitative research: Interpretive and critical approaches. Thousand Oaks, CA: Sage.

Wilson, P. (2007). Gear Picks. The Ottawa Citizen, F.4. Retrieved April 29, 2012, from ProQuest database.

Wong, M. (2010). Guanxi management as complex adaptive systems: A case study of Taiwanese ODI in China. *Journal of Business Ethics, 91*, 419-432. doi:10.1007/s10551-009-0093-1

Xu, Q., Chen, J., Xie, Z., Liu, J., Zheng, G., & Wang, Y. (2006). Total innovation management: A novel paradigm of innovation management in the 21st century. *Journal of Technology Transfer, 32*, 9-25.

Yan, Z. (2007). A new approach to studying complex systems. *Systems Research & Behavioral Science, 24*, 403-416. doi:10.1002/sres.843

Yan, Z., & Yan, X. (2010). A revolution in the field of systems thinking: A review of Checkland's system thinking. *Systems Research & Behavioral Science, 27*, 140-155. doi:10.1002/sres.1021

Yeo, R. K. (2009). Electronic government as a strategic intervention in organizational change processes. *Journal of Change Management, 9*, 271-304.

Yin, R. K. (2009). *Case study research: Design and methods* (4th ed., Vol. 5). Thousand Oaks, CA: Sage.

Yoon, S.-W., & Kuchinke, K. P. (2005). Systems Theory and Technology: Lenses to Analyze an Organization. *Performance Improvement, 44*(4), 15-20.